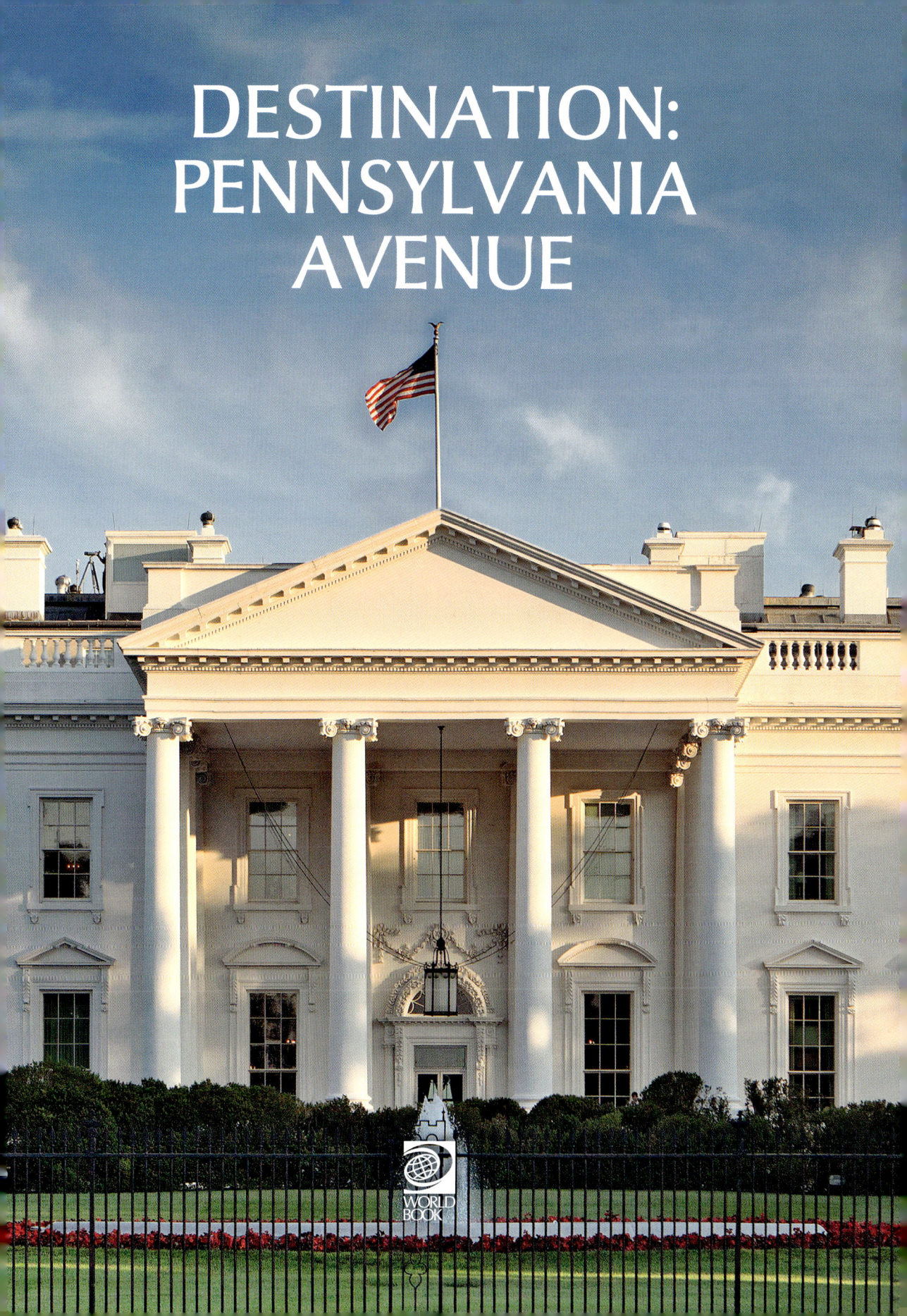

World Book, Inc.
180 North LaSalle Street
Suite 900
Chicago, Illinois 60601
USA

For information about other World Book publications, visit our website at **www.worldbook.com** or call **1-800-WORLDBK (967-5325)**.
For information about sales to schools and libraries, call 1-800-975-3250 (United States),
or 1-800-837-5365 (Canada).

© 2021 World Book, Inc. All rights reserved. This volume may not be reproduced in whole or in part in any form without prior written permission from the publisher.

WORLD BOOK and the GLOBE DEVICE are registered trademarks or trademarks of World Book, Inc.

STAFF

Executive Committee
President: Geoff Broderick
Vice President, Finance: Donald D. Keller
Vice President, Marketing: Jean Lin
Vice President, International Sales:
 Maksim Rutenberg
Vice President, Technology: Jason Dole
Vice President, Customer Success:
 Jade Lewandowski
Director, Editorial: Tom Evans
Director, Human Resources: Bev Ecker

Editorial
Manager: Kristina A. Vaicikonis
Writers/Senior Editors:
 Shawn Brennan,
 Kenneth J. Shenkman
Proofreader/Indexer: Nathalie Strassheim

Graphics and Design
Coordinator, Design Development and
 Production: Brenda Tropinski
Media Researcher: Rosalia Bledsoe

Marketing
Marketing Analyst: Zofia Kulik
Marketing Coordinator: Bri Milker

Library of Congress Cataloging-in-Publication Data for this volume has been applied for.

Destination: Pennsylvania Avenue
ISBN: 978-0-7166-3705-9 (hc.)
ISBN: 978-0-7166-3706-6 (e-book)

Printed in USA by Corporate Graphics
1st printing March 2021

CONTENTS

Introduction 4
The American President 6
Roads to the White House 12
HOW DOES THE PRESIDENT GET ELECTED? 14
    Winning the Nomination 16
    National Conventions 20
    Campaigning 22
    Time to Vote! 26
    The Electoral College 34
The Vice President: A Heartbeat Away 40
Presidential Transition 46
Inauguration Day 48
Presidential Legacy 52
Hail to the Chief: The 46 U.S. Presidents 54
Quiz: What Did You Learn About the Presidents? 55
President Joe Biden Biography 56
Index 62
Acknowledgments/Quiz Answers 64

INTRODUCTION

The president of the United States is often considered the most powerful elected official in the world. In spite of the fact that the framers of the Constitution listed all the powers of the president in just a few paragraphs, the president today occupies a uniquely powerful position. Over the years, events and presidential personalities have molded the office of the presidency, so that the president has become truly a world leader, as well as leader of the nation.

The president and vice president of the United States are the only U.S. officials elected by voters throughout the country. Unlike senators or governors or mayors, the president is elected to serve all Americans and stands as the most visible symbol of the nation. Americans look to their president to solve complicated national problems, to lead them through crises, and to set priorities and policies that will affect their everyday lives in many ways. Although the responsibilities for governing the nation are largely in the hands of thousands of elected and appointed officials, it is the president who stands in the spotlight of national attention. When government policies are successful, it is the president who often enjoys the praise and thanks of the nation. But the president is also the person who shoulders much of the blame when government policies fail to produce desired results.

On the morning of Jan. 20, 2021, Donald J. Trump left the White House for the last time as president. A few hours later, at the U.S. Capitol, Chief Justice John Roberts swore in Joseph R. Biden, Jr., as the 46th president of the United States. The election capped off the most turbulent year in generations. For years to come, historians will attempt to make sense of the events of 2020. The United States had already been polarized politically, but a series of historic challenges compounded this division. The COVID-19 pandemic claimed more than 400,000 American lives by year's end. Millions lost their jobs. Protests following the killings, by police, of George Floyd and other Black Americans produced moments of solidarity, anguish, and unrest. Demonstrations against pandemic-inspired business restrictions drew both sympathy and condemnation. Americans viewed each of these events through a political lens.

By the start of 2020, Democratic presidential hopefuls had already participated in many debates. President Trump, presiding over a strong economy, looked like an incumbent who would be tough to unseat. Organizers of both parties helped register millions of new voters. But by March, coronavirus patients overwhelmed hospitals, and the world became familiar with such new terms as *lockdown*, *social distancing*, and *PPE*—personal protective equipment, worn to help keep wearers free of infection. State election officials scrambled to adapt to the pandemic era, reorganizing primary contests and expanding the availability of vote by mail.

The election brought out record numbers of voters: 81 million for Biden and 74 million for Trump. Close tallies in a number of swing states triggered recounts, and Trump filed dozens of unsuccessful lawsuits aiming to overturn the results. Long after the results were certified, Trump refused to concede. Many Trump supporters embraced his narrative about a stolen election. Some of his most strident followers even stormed the U.S. Capitol. The president, accused of encouraging an insurrection, was tried for impeachment after he left office—making him the only president to be impeached twice. Trump was *acquitted* (found not guilty) both times.

How could such things happen in the United States? World Book's *Destination: Pennsylvania Avenue* separates fact from fiction, describing the presidential election process from the primaries and caucuses to Inauguration Day, and explains the unique challenges and historical significance of the 2020 election. Framed within historical context, *Destination: Pennsylvania Avenue* answers the important questions—posed in the classroom and around the dinner table—about the unprecedented election year that was.

THE AMERICAN PRESIDENT

Abraham Lincoln

A UNIQUE LEADER

As leader of a nation of great wealth and military strength, the president of the United States plays an important role in shaping world events. What the president thinks, says, and does affects everyone throughout the world. And the president's job is unique. Like a king or queen, the president is chief of state. Like a prime minister, the chief executive heads the U.S. government and conducts foreign policy. Like a general, the president is commander in chief of the armed forces.

President Harry S. Truman

In addition, the president proposes legislation to Congress and heads a major political party. While some officials pass along responsibility or "pass the buck," President Harry S. Truman believed it is the job of the president to make decisions and take the ultimate responsibility for those decisions. He kept a sign on his desk that read, "The Buck Stops Here."

The U.S. president today is the center of attention of the media of both the United States and the rest of the world. Presidential words and actions are repeated around the globe on radio, on television, on the internet, and in newspapers and magazines in hundreds of languages. In most other countries, the name and face of the president of the United States is as familiar to the people as the names and faces of their own leaders. The president is truly a world leader as well as the leader of the U.S. government.

As powerful as the role of president of the United States is, however, there are limits to what the president can do. The Constitution establishes a strict separation of powers among the executive, legislative, and judicial branches of the federal government. The president cannot directly control Congress or the courts. And these branches of the government can limit the president's ability to act.

Probably the greatest limitation on the president's power resides in the people. Every four years, the voters choose their president. The president and the vice president are the only public officials in the United States elected on a nationwide basis. In a sense, the president represents all the people, and their opinion counts. Only with the confidence of the people can the president perform the most important role of office—that of leadership.

Joe Biden formally launches his 2020 presidential campaign during a rally on May 18, 2019, at Eakins Oval in Pennsylvania.

THE AMERICAN PRESIDENT

THE PRESIDENT'S UNIQUE DUTIES

The U.S. president has many different and important duties. In most other countries, these various functions are carried out by more than one person. But in the United States, they are all the president's responsibility. These duties can be organized into seven basic roles:

1. **Chief of state.** As chief of state, the president conducts ceremonial affairs, as royalty would do in nations ruled by monarchs. The president presides at ceremonies at home and travels to other countries on state visits.

2. **Chief executive.** As chief executive, the president has four main duties. They are (1) to enforce federal laws, treaties, and federal court rulings; (2) to develop federal policies; (3) to prepare the national budget; and (4) to appoint federal officials.

3. **Foreign policy director.** As foreign policy director, the president shares the duty of making foreign policy with Congress. But the president holds the most important position in international affairs.

4. **Commander in chief.** As commander in chief of the armed forces, the president is responsible for national defense in peace or war. This post symbolizes the supremacy of civilian authority over military authority in the United States.

5. **Legislative leader.** The president as legislative leader proposes new laws for congressional consideration and urges Congress to act on the proposals.

6. **Political leader.** Presidents use the position as head of their political party to influence members of Congress to take stands on foreign and domestic issues. Legislators, however, owe loyalty to state and local party organizations and to the voters who must reelect them. They may vote against a bill favored by the president if it meets with opposition at home.

President Franklin D. Roosevelt addressed the nation over the radio in his "fireside chats." These informal reports not only kept the American people informed, but they also helped to boost morale during the Great Depression of the 1930's and World War II (1939-1945). The fireside chats also enabled Roosevelt to gain widespread support for his programs.

7. **Popular leader.** The president and the American people have a special relationship. The people rely on the chief executive to serve the interests of the entire nation ahead of those of any state or citizen. In turn, the president depends on public support to help push programs through Congress. The president uses many methods to communicate with the public and provide strong national leadership. These methods include radio, television, press conferences, and social media.

President John F. Kennedy was a master of press conferences. He often invited editors and reporters to special White House meetings for background briefings and casual conversation. Kennedy began the practice of appearing live on television screens—he gave the first televised press conference in 1961. Since then, all other presidents have followed his example.

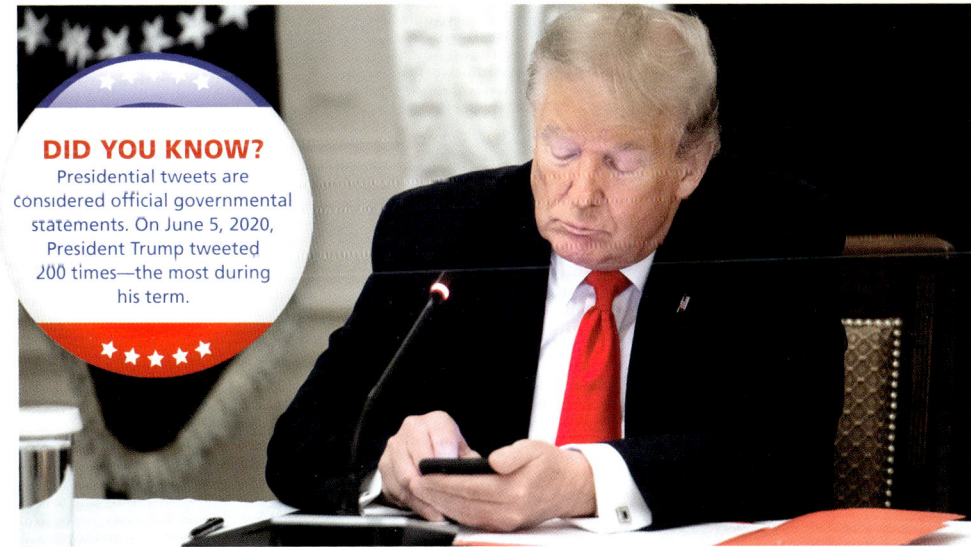

DID YOU KNOW?
Presidential tweets are considered official governmental statements. On June 5, 2020, President Trump tweeted 200 times—the most during his term.

President Donald J. Trump often used the social media site Twitter to reach his supporters directly.

9

THE AMERICAN PRESIDENT

President Ronald Reagan is sworn into office for his second term in 1985. As he takes the oath of office, he places his hand on a Bible held by his wife, Nancy Reagan.

LEGAL QUALIFICATIONS, TERMS, AND SALARY

Legal qualifications. The Constitution establishes only three qualifications for a president. A president must:
1. Be at least 35 years old.
2. Have lived in the United States for at least 14 years.
3. Be a natural-born citizen.

Courts have never decided whether a person born abroad to American parents could serve as president of the United States. However, many scholars believe that such a person would be considered a natural-born citizen.

Term of office. The president is elected to a four-year term. The 22nd Amendment to the Constitution provides that no one may be elected president more than twice. Nobody who has served as president for more than two years of someone else's term may be elected more than once.

The Constitution allows Congress to remove a president from office. The president first must be *impeached* (charged with wrongdoing) by a majority vote of the House of Representatives. Then, the Senate, with the chief justice of the United States serving as presiding officer, tries the president on the charges. Removal from office requires conviction by a two-thirds vote of the Senate.

Only three presidents—Andrew Johnson, Bill Clinton, and Donald J. Trump—have been impeached (Trump twice). All were *acquitted* (found not guilty) by the Senate. Congress also considered articles of impeachment against Richard Nixon. After those articles were approved by the House Judiciary Committee, Nixon resigned from office.

Salary and other allowances. The president receives a salary of $400,000 a year. The chief executive also gets $50,000 annually for expenses, plus allowances for staff, travel, and maintenance of the White House. Congress establishes all these amounts. After leaving office, a president qualifies for a basic pension.

Q&A

HOW MANY PRESIDENTS WERE ELECTED TO ONLY ONE TERM?

Of the 46 presidents who have held office since 1789, only 11 (excluding those who died in office or did not seek reelection) have served one term:

1797–1801	John Adams
1825–1829	John Quincy Adams
1837–1841	Martin Van Buren
1853–1857	Franklin Pierce
1865–1869	Andrew Johnson
1881–1885	Chester Arthur
1889–1893	Benjamin Harrison
1909–1913	William Howard Taft
1977–1981	Jimmy Carter
1989–1993	George H. W. Bush
2017–2021	Donald J. Trump

Grover Cleveland was the only president to win a second term that did not directly follow the first: he won in 1884, lost in 1888, and won in 1892.

DID YOU KNOW?
Franklin D. Roosevelt is the only president to be elected four times. He served from 1933 to 1945. In 1951, the 22nd Amendment to the Constitution was approved. It provided that no one may be elected president more than twice.

JUST THE FACTS

Youngest president:
Theodore Roosevelt, 42, in 1901; took office when President William McKinley was assassinated

Youngest elected president:
John F. Kennedy, 43, in 1960

Oldest elected president:
Joe Biden, 77, in 2020

Theodore Roosevelt

ROADS TO THE WHITE HOUSE

Presidential election. The chief road to the White House is the presidential election. The Constitution requires that presidential elections be held every four years.

Other roads to the White House. However, a person may become president of the United States in several other ways as well. These procedures are established by Article II of the Constitution; the 12th and 20th amendments; and the Presidential Succession Act.

Article II provides that the vice president becomes president whenever the president dies, resigns, is removed from office, or cannot fulfill the duties of the presidency. Nine vice presidents became president by filling a vacancy. One of them, Gerald R. Ford, followed an unusual route to the White House. President Richard M. Nixon nominated him to succeed Spiro T. Agnew, who had resigned as vice president in 1973. In 1974, Nixon resigned as president,

Gerald Ford, *left,* was the only vice president of the United States to become president upon the resignation of a chief executive. Richard M. Nixon resigned as president on Aug. 9, 1974, and Ford took office that same day.

and Ford succeeded him. Ford was the only president who was not elected to either the vice presidency or the presidency.

The 12th Amendment permits Congress to act if no candidate for president wins a majority of the electoral votes. Then, the House of Representatives chooses the president. Each state delegation casts one vote. The House has elected two presidents, Thomas Jefferson in 1801 and John Quincy Adams in 1825.

George W. Bush   Al Gore

In 2000, the presidential election between George W. Bush and Al Gore was so close that it was virtually tied. However, the House of Representatives did not choose the winning candidate. Bush had won the state of Florida by fewer than 1,800 votes, and Gore requested a court-ordered recount of the votes. In the case of *Bush v. Gore*, the U.S. Supreme Court stopped the recount. That court ruling established Bush as the winner of the election.

The 20th Amendment states that if the Electoral College chooses a president-elect who then dies before the inauguration, the vice president-elect becomes president. This provision has never been applied. If a presidential candidate dies before the Electoral College meets, leaders of the candidate's party may select a new presidential candidate for their party. The college would then vote on that selection.

The Presidential Succession Act permits other high government officials to become president if vacancies exist in both the presidency and the vice presidency. Next in line is the speaker of the House. Then comes the *president pro tempore* (temporary president) of the Senate, usually the majority party member who has served the longest in the Senate. Next are members of the important presidential advisory group that is known as the Cabinet, with the secretary of state first. The Succession Act has never been applied.

Order of Presidential Succession
1. Vice President
2. Speaker of the House
3. President Pro Tempore of the Senate
4. Secretary of State
5. Secretary of the Treasury
6. Secretary of Defense
7. Attorney General
8. Secretary of the Interior
9. Secretary of Agriculture
10. Secretary of Commerce
11. Secretary of Labor
12. Secretary of Health and Human Services
13. Secretary of Housing and Urban Development
14. Secretary of Transportation
15. Secretary of Energy
16. Secretary of Education
17. Secretary of Veterans Affairs
18. Secretary of Homeland Security

HOW DOES THE PRESIDENT GET ELECTED?

U.S. CONSTITUTION'S REQUIREMENTS FOR A PRESIDENTIAL CANDIDATE

☑ NATURAL-BORN CITIZEN   ☑ MINIMUM AGE 35 YEARS   ☑ U.S. RESIDEN 14 YEARS

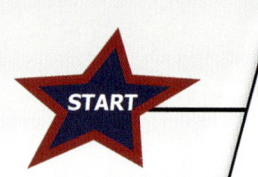

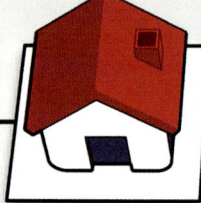

STEP 2 NATIONAL CONVENTIONS

At each convention, the presidential candidate chooses a running mate (vice presidential candidate).

Each party holds a national convention to select a final presidential nominee.

The presidential candidates campaign throughout the country to win the support of the general population.

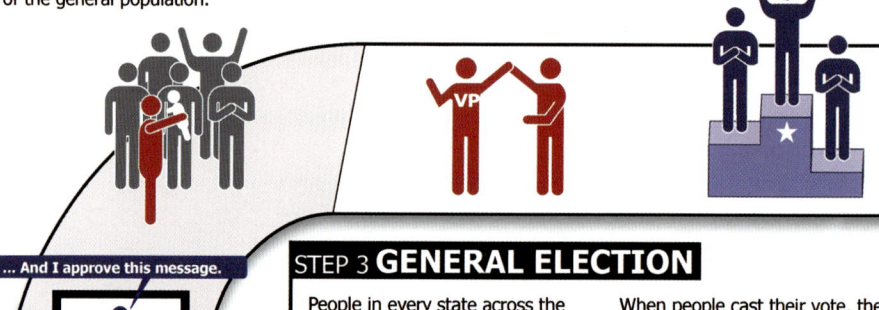

STEP 3 GENERAL ELECTION

People in every state across the country vote for one president and vice president.

When people cast their vote, they are actually voting for a group of people called **electors**.

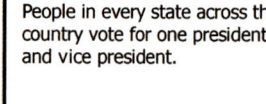

DEFINITIONS

Caucus: A meeting of the local members of a political party to select delegates to the national party convention. A caucus is a substitute for a primary election.

Delegate: A person authorized to represent others as an elected representative to a political party conference.

Elector: A member of the electoral college.

Electoral College: The voters of each state, and the District of Columbia, vote for electors to be the authorized constitutional members in a presidential election.

Natural-Born Citizen: Someone born with U.S. citizenship includes any child born "in" the United States, the children of United States citizens born abroad, and those born abroad of one citizen parent.

Primary: An election where voters select candidates for an upcoming general election. Winning candidates will have delegates sent to the national party convention as their party's U.S. presidential nominee.

14

Follow the campaign trail to see how a citizen goes from being a candidate to being sworn in as the most powerful elected official in the world. Go through the primaries and on to the national political convention, the popular vote in November, and finally the Electoral College vote—the end of a long and difficult path. Inauguration Day takes place in January, when the elected president's new term begins.

STEP 1 PRIMARIES AND CAUCUSES

There are many people who want to be president, each with their own ideas about how government should work.

People with similar ideas belong to the same political party. This is where primaries and caucuses come in.

Candidates from each political party campaign through the country to win the favor of their party members.

IN A PRIMARY
Party members vote for the best candidate that will represent them in the general election.

IN A CAUCUS
Party members select the best candidate through a series of discussions and votes.

STEP 4 ELECTORAL COLLEGE

In the electoral college system, each state gets a certain number of electors based on its representation in Congress.

Each elector casts one vote following the general election, and the candidate who gets more than half (270) wins.

538 ELECTORAL VOTES

270 VOTES

The newly elected president and vice president are inaugurated in January.

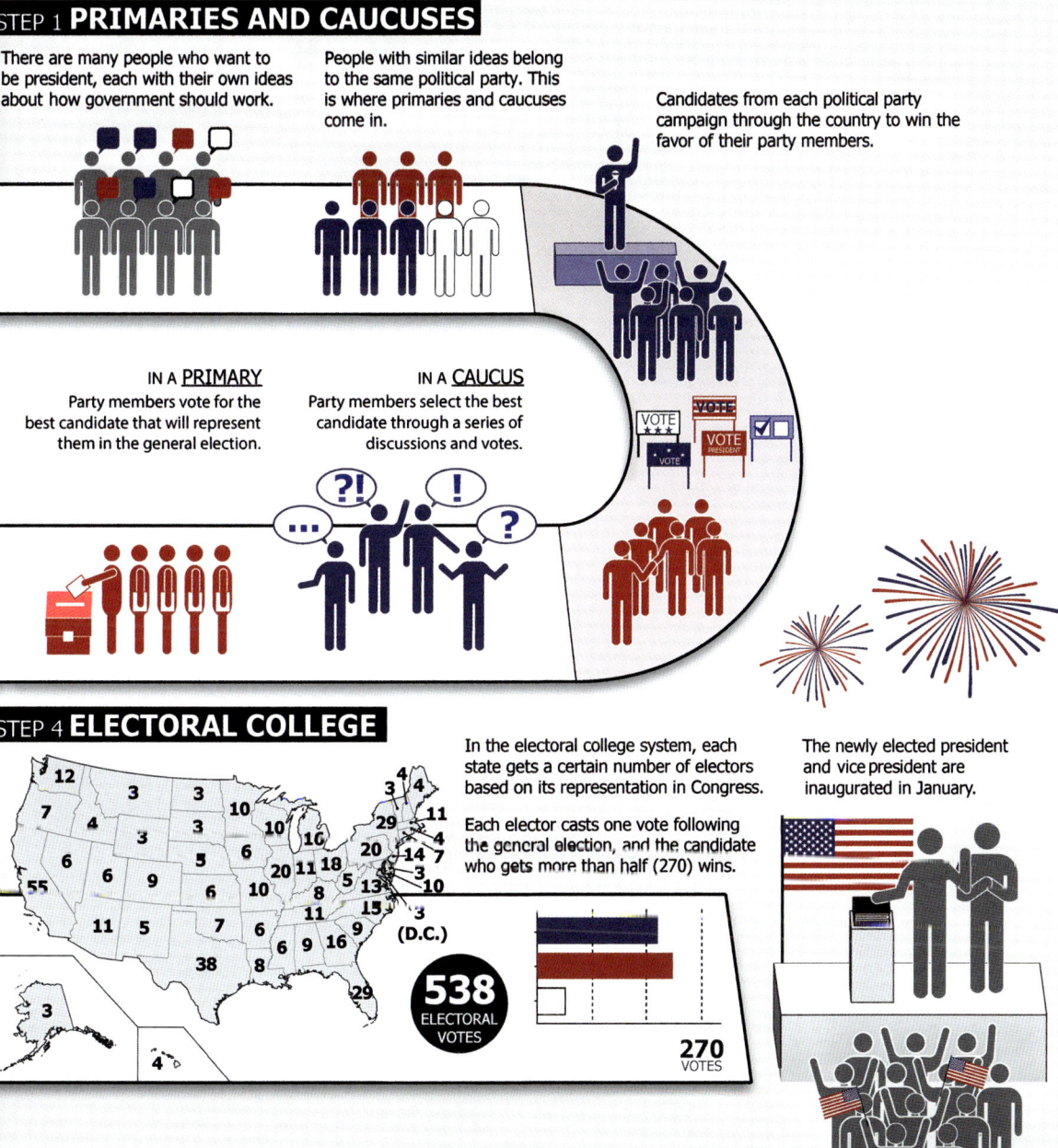

15

HOW DOES THE PRESIDENT GET ELECTED?
WINNING THE NOMINATION

Republican candidate Dwight D. Eisenhower campaigns for president in 1952.

POLITICAL PARTIES

Most top presidential candidates must first compete against fellow political party members to win the party's presidential nomination. The Democratic and Republican parties are the two main political parties in the United States.

Political parties are absolutely necessary to democratic government. Most modern democracies are *representative* democracies. That is, the people elect representatives to act as their agents in making and enforcing laws. In a representative democracy, some means is needed for nominating candidates for public office and for selecting issues for public debate. Political parties perform these functions. At election time, the people vote into office the candidates of their choice. Political parties are voluntary organizations and want as many members as possible. Some of these parties have rules and membership dues. Others have practically no rules and require no dues.

Political parties perform several important tasks:
1. They select candidates to run for public office.
2. They help organize the government.
3. They provide opposition to the party in power.
4. They raise funds to conduct election campaigns.

Other functions of parties in democratic countries include informing voters about public affairs and about problems that need government action.

DID YOU KNOW?
George Washington was the only president who did not belong to a party and who was unanimously elected—even though he did not want the job.

DONKEYS VS. ELEPHANTS?

The donkey is a popular symbol of the Democratic Party in the United States, and the elephant is a symbol of the Republican Party. The American political cartoonist Thomas Nast (1840-1902) popularized the symbols while working at the magazine *Harper's Weekly*. Through political cartoons that featured a variety of animals, Nast illustrated—both literally and figuratively—that politics is as messy and chaotic as a circus.

The Democratic donkey is believed to have first been used during the 1828 presidential campaign. The Democratic candidate Andrew Jackson—who went on to win the presidency that year—used the symbol on his posters, in defiance of opponents who had unflatteringly compared him to a type of donkey.

Historians believe that Nast's 1874 cartoon "The Third Term Panic" popularized the elephant as a symbol of the Republican Party. In the cartoon, a donkey disguised as a lion chases several animals. An elephant labeled "Republican Vote" lumbers toward a pit labeled "inflation" and "chaos." Nast said the elephant depicted the confused creature that was the Republican Party at that time.

Nast is also known for his work during the American Civil War (1861-1865), when his political cartoons influenced public opinion in favor of the North. The donkey and the elephant are not the only American symbols associated with Nast. He is credited with creating the present-day image of Santa Claus in sketches that appeared in *Harper's Weekly* in the 1860's.

WINNING THE NOMINATION

PRIMARIES AND CAUCUSES

Both parties hold presidential *primaries* or *caucuses* in the first half of the election year to select their candidates.

A primary is an election in which members of a political party choose candidates for office. The presidential primary is used in over half of the states to choose delegates to the national party conventions. Each candidate who enters the election lists a slate of delegates who have promised to support the candidate at the convention. The party members show their choice for the presidential nomination by voting for the slate of delegates committed to that candidate. Primaries that select about two-thirds of the delegates are held in the first six months of presidential election years.

A caucus is a meeting of members or leaders of a political party to make plans, choose candidates, or decide how to vote. The *participatory caucus* is used in the United States in presidential election years. The best-known participatory caucuses are those held in Iowa by the Republican and Democratic parties. The Iowa caucuses are the first major events in a series of state caucuses and primary elections that end in the nomination of each party's presidential candidate. For this reason, the Iowa caucuses receive a great deal of coverage from newspapers, television, and other media.

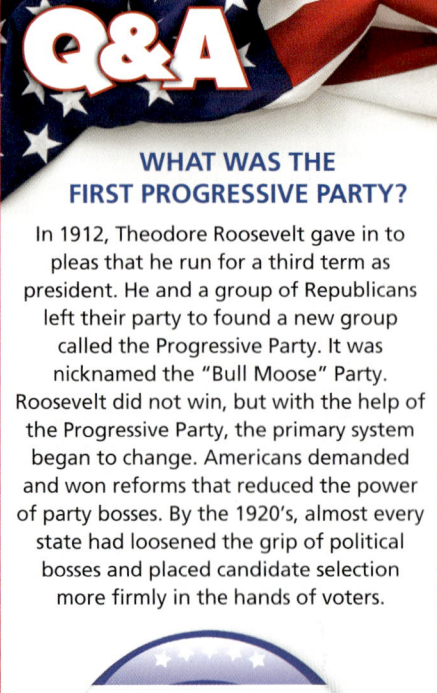

Q&A

WHAT WAS THE FIRST PROGRESSIVE PARTY?

In 1912, Theodore Roosevelt gave in to pleas that he run for a third term as president. He and a group of Republicans left their party to found a new group called the Progressive Party. It was nicknamed the "Bull Moose" Party. Roosevelt did not win, but with the help of the Progressive Party, the primary system began to change. Americans demanded and won reforms that reduced the power of party bosses. By the 1920's, almost every state had loosened the grip of political bosses and placed candidate selection more firmly in the hands of voters.

DID YOU KNOW?
Theodore Roosevelt's Progressive Party was called the Bull Moose Party. The name came from Roosevelt's reply when a reporter asked how he felt. "I feel as strong as a bull moose," he said.

JUST THE FACTS
- Since 1976, two people have gone on to win the presidency after losing both the Iowa caucus and the New Hampshire primary: Democrats Bill Clinton, in 1992, and Joe Biden, in 2020.
- Also since 1976, no Republican has become the presidential nominee without winning either Iowa or New Hampshire.

YOU'RE HIRED! 2020'S ULTIMATE JOB SEARCH

In 2019, at the start of the 2020 election cycle, Democrats fielded 28 candidates for the nomination—a record since the current system of caucuses and primaries took shape in 1972. In 2016, a then-record 17 Republican candidates sought the nomination. But only 4, including President Trump, entered the 2020 campaign.

The Democratic National Committee (DNC) held eleven presidential primary debates. The party weighed candidates' fundraising and polling numbers in determining who would qualify to appear in each of the televised events.

By March 2020, 21 Democrats had dropped out of the race. The 7 remaining candidates were: former Vice President Joe Biden; Senators Elizabeth Warren of Massachusetts, Amy Klobuchar of Minnesota, and Bernie Sanders of Vermont; U.S. Representative Tulsi Gabbard of Hawaii; and former mayors Pete Buttigieg of South Bend, Indiana, and Michael Bloomberg of New York City.

Candidates continued to drop out of the race and only two—Biden and Sanders—qualified for the final debate on March 15. About that time, COVID-19 was labeled a pandemic and had spread throughout the country. Hospitals approached capacity and authorities issued stay-at-home orders to slow the spread of the disease. Candidates canceled rallies and suspended door-to-door campaigning. Candidates struggled to garner news coverage to amplify their messages. Sanders ended his campaign in April, and Biden became the party's presumptive nominee.

Other than the president, Republican candidates included former Massachusetts Governor William Weld; radio host and former Congressman Joe Walsh of Illinois; and former Governor and Congressman Mark Sanford of South Carolina. Trump coasted to victory and earned enough delegates needed to win the Republican nomination on March 17.

Candidates of other parties included Libertarian Jo Jorgensen of South Carolina, a university professor; and the Green Party's Howie Hawkins, an environmental activist from New York. Also competing was hip-hop star and fashion mogul Kanye West, who claimed he was just "walking" for president, not running, as a candidate for the "Birthday Party."

Competitors for the Democratic presidential nomination included, *from left to right,* philanthropist Tom Steyer; Massachusetts Senator Elizabeth Warren; former Vice President Joe Biden; Vermont Senator Bernie Sanders; former mayor of South Bend, Indiana, Pete Buttigieg; and Minnesota Senator Amy Klobuchar. The candidates are shown at the seventh Democratic primary debate of the 2020 season, at Drake University in Des Moines, Iowa, on January 14.

George H. W. Bush, 1988 Republican Convention

HOW DOES THE PRESIDENT GET ELECTED?
NATIONAL CONVENTIONS

After the primaries and caucuses, each party holds a national *convention* to nominate its presidential candidate. A convention is a gathering at which major political parties in the United States formally nominate their candidates for president and vice president. The Democratic and Republican national conventions are four-day events that take place every four years. The two conventions are held at separate times during the summer of each presidential election year. They are typically held in separate cities, and in different cities from year to year.

The Democratic and Republican conventions are lively spectacles. Millions of Americans watch them on television. Delegates wave banners and cheer wildly to support their choice for president. Huge crowds gather at each convention. The people in attendance include thousands of party delegates, who nominate a candidate they hope can win the presidential election the following November. An even larger number of magazine, newspaper, radio, and television reporters come to the convention. They provide coverage of the gathering for millions of voters throughout the nation. Many other people attend conventions, including *lobbyists* (representatives of interest groups), people who contribute money to the party or its candidates, and alternate delegates.

DID YOU KNOW?
At the Democratic presidential convention of 1844, James K. Polk became the first "dark horse," or unexpected, candidate. He was nominated as a result of a compromise because the delegates at the convention could not agree on former President Martin Van Buren or his rival.

2020 CONVENTIONS IN A COVID WORLD

In mid-August 2020, prior to the Democratic National Convention, former Vice President Joe Biden named California Senator Kamala Harris to be his running mate. The convention took place in Milwaukee from August 17 to 20. Because of the ongoing pandemic, convention speeches occurred "virtually"—that is, via video transmission—without in-person attendees. Biden accepted the nomination on August 20, when he asked voters, "with love and hope and light, [to] join in the battle for the soul of our nation."

The Republican National Convention took place in a scaled-down format in late August in Charlotte, North Carolina. Trump accepted the party's nomination during a televised rally held on the White House lawn on August 27. During the event, Trump proclaimed, "At no time before have voters faced a clearer choice between two parties, two visions, two philosophies, or two agendas. This election will decide whether we save the American Dream or whether we allow a socialist agenda to demolish our cherished destiny."

Former Vice President Joe Biden, *lower left,* Senator Kamala Harris, *lower right,* and their spouses interact with convention viewers from a Wilmington, Delaware, stage on Aug. 20, 2020. Much of the convention took place in Milwaukee, Wisconsin, without in-person attendees.

President Donald J. Trump, *above center,* accepts the Republican nomination for president on the South Lawn of the White House in Washington, D.C., on Aug. 27, 2020.

HOW DOES THE PRESIDENT GET ELECTED?
CAMPAIGNING

After the conventions, the presidential nominees campaign across the nation. Election campaigns usually include numerous advertisements, use of social media, public appearances, interviews, speeches, and debates. Candidates for president face many challenges. They must raise millions of dollars for campaign expenses, attract many volunteers, and gain the support of voters throughout the country.

   A presidential campaign may involve as many as 500 paid staff members and hundreds of thousands of volunteers. A campaign director heads the organization and coordinates activities. Other officials of a large campaign may include a general manager, a research director, a finance director, and a *media director,* who supervises advertising and publicity. Most candidates make frequent public appearances. Specialists called *advance people* may travel ahead to make arrangements, and professional political consultants usually help plan and conduct various operations. For example, many candidates employ a polling organization to take public opinion polls. Many hire marketing and messaging specialists to create advertisements and send messages that target likely voters. Mail, email, telephone, and social media are frequently employed by campaigns. Volunteers may distribute leaflets, prepare mailings, call voters, and perform many other important tasks. The leadership, organization, and support of a campaign are critical to a candidate's success.

CAMPAIGNING DURING A PANDEMIC

Nominating campaigns in 2020 began rather conventionally. Observers tracking coronavirus outbreaks in China and Italy, however, began to expect that the 2020 campaign—and life in general—might soon not resemble anything conventional for months to come.

The public health crisis forced many businesses to close and sent unemployment figures soaring. Polls showed that the coronavirus and handling of relief efforts had become the top concern of voters.

Campaigns entered something of a hibernation period during the lockdown months of spring. In June, Trump returned to the campaign trail, holding a rally at an indoor arena in Tulsa, Oklahoma. With official events, press conferences, and other rallies occurring primarily outdoors, Trump had little trouble staying in the news. For his part, Biden conducted interviews with local news media via a studio constructed in the basement of his Delaware home.

Trump invested considerable reelection funds in a sophisticated website and smartphone app, helping the campaign reach, register, and rally supporters. After officially accepting the Republican nomination in August, Trump held an outdoor rally from the White House lawn. The pandemic itself, however, became the news narrative in October, when the president, First Lady Melania, and their son Barron, as well as several White House staffers, contracted the virus.

Biden held a number of outdoor events, including drive-in rallies, for limited numbers of attendees. Campaign coordinators conducted extensive phone, text, mail, and email outreach and employed the video communications platform Zoom to organize with volunteers. The Democratic National Convention in August was a surreal affair, conducted without in-person attendees.

Ultimately, the pandemic altered campaigning in much the same way it upended everyday life throughout the world. In some small ways, however, the candidates brought back the campaigns of yesteryear. Politicking from their homes, they called to mind the "front porch" campaigns of James A. Garfield, Benjamin Harrison, William McKinley, and Warren Harding.

President Donald J. Trump speaks at a campaign rally at the Des Moines International Airport in Iowa on Oct. 14, 2020.

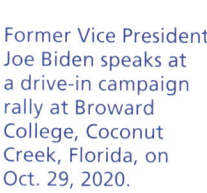

Former Vice President Joe Biden speaks at a drive-in campaign rally at Broward College, Coconut Creek, Florida, on Oct. 29, 2020.

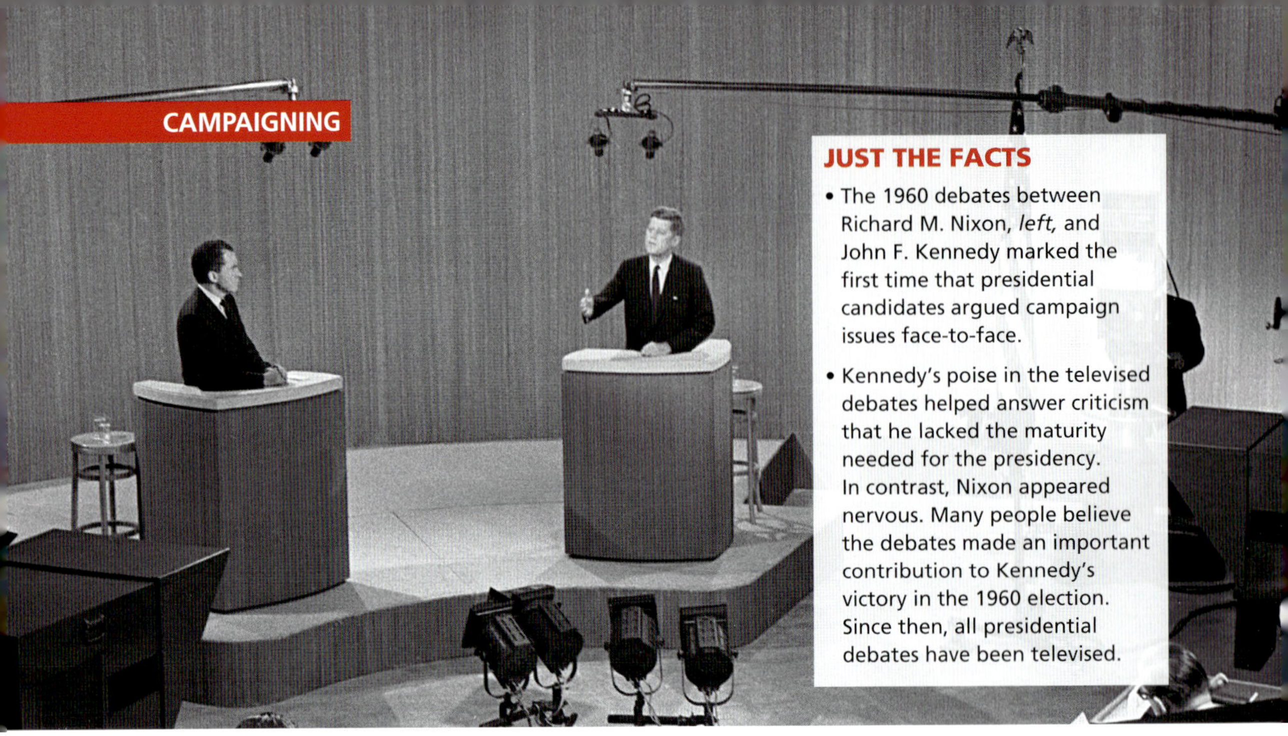

CAMPAIGNING

JUST THE FACTS
- The 1960 debates between Richard M. Nixon, *left,* and John F. Kennedy marked the first time that presidential candidates argued campaign issues face-to-face.
- Kennedy's poise in the televised debates helped answer criticism that he lacked the maturity needed for the presidency. In contrast, Nixon appeared nervous. Many people believe the debates made an important contribution to Kennedy's victory in the 1960 election. Since then, all presidential debates have been televised.

Campaign funds are necessary to pay personnel and to finance advertising, travel, and other needs. The chief sources of funds are personal solicitations, appeals by direct mail, internet contributions, fund-raising events, and *matching funds.* Matching funds from the federal government are available to presidential candidates if contributions to their campaign meet certain requirements. Bank loans are also a common source of campaign money. Campaign finance laws have greatly affected campaign financing and spending in the United States.

The campaign continues until Election Day, the first Tuesday after the first Monday in November. As the election approaches, the pace of the campaign quickens. Candidates usually issue more frequent news releases and increase advertising. Campaign workers step up efforts to persuade voters to go to the polls and vote for their candidate.

DID YOU KNOW?
The 2020 United States elections were the most expensive in history. The elections cost over $14 billion—twice as much as the last election cycle. Joe Biden raised over $1 billion from donors—the first presidential candidate to do so.

The first presidential debate between Joe Biden and Donald J. Trump was held on Sept. 29, 2020, at Case Western Reserve University in Cleveland, Ohio.

DIVISION 2020

The challenges America faced in 2020 made it seem that the country was more divided than ever. Americans faced a common foe in a historic pandemic. But politics, protests, and, at times, violence and lawlessness pitted neighbor against neighbor.

Some 300,000 U.S. veterans of World War II (1939-1945) were alive at the start of 2020. Many consider their generation, including the millions who toiled on the home front during the war, to be the last to have truly experienced collective, national sacrifice in the name of the public good. The coronavirus, more than 600 times deadlier for people age 85 and over, accelerated the loss of thousands of their generation, robbing the nation of their voices and their example. What they strove for encompassed the idea of *American exceptionalism*—that is, the idea that American ideals of liberty and equality are an inspiration to the world. This notion sometimes appeared quaint and antiquated during the political battles of 2020.

Late in the spring, protests and counterprotests, accompanied at times by unrest sparked by criminals and opportunists, shattered the silence of pandemic lockdowns. News commentators, politicians, and even those suspected to be in the employ of foreign nations reduced stories on police misconduct, protests, and the ongoing pandemic to simple *memes*—that is, ideas that easily spread from person to person. Few 2020 news items seemed to escape the "us vs. them" model, and social media feeds, organized by seldom-understood algorithms, delivered content that reinforced their followers' core beliefs and biases. The virus kept people from interacting with others and left many confined in smaller quarters, poring over screens.

During this time of true uncertainty, the power of *anonymity*—being of unknown identity—contributed to a common sense of unease. Faceless, anonymous actors trolled social media, spreading lies and fear. Face masks, once the reserve of surgeons and bank robbers, became mandatory apparel, as many sought to protect themselves and their neighbors. But at an unruly demonstration, neither law enforcement officers nor the public could tell who was a protester, a bystander, a common criminal, or a sophisticated one. People's political leanings colored their perceptions.

The election proved contentious, and its aftermath jarring. Leaders of the government, schools, and houses of worship were left with serious issues to consider. What steps could be taken to encourage voting, protect electoral systems, and restore faith in the electoral process? How should people speak to neighbors, friends, and family about their political differences? What people and news sources can be trusted? How can propaganda, on both sides, be identified? How do people use selective truths to tell an incomplete or slanted story? Who benefits from fueling unrest, and who suffers?

Public opinion polls showed that the majority of supporters of both parties largely agreed on many issues, such as the right to clean air and water, a good education, and a government that protects people's freedoms. But not everyone, of course, defined *freedom* in the same terms.

THE FEDERALIST, NO. 10: JAMES MADISON WARNED AGAINST FACTIONS

During the debates over the Constitution, American statesman James Madison expressed concerns over the emergence of *factions*—political groups that, he believed, united for narrow and unjust goals that curtail the rights of other citizens. Contributing to a series of essays called *The Federalist,* Madison described how factions had contributed to the destruction of past governments. He supported a system of separation of powers and checks and balances to protect citizens from factions within the government.

HOW DOES THE PRESIDENT GET ELECTED?
TIME TO VOTE!

DID YOU KNOW?
In 1997, Texas passed a bill to allow NASA astronauts to vote from space! Astronauts fill out a standard mail-in form ahead of launch and email it from space through NASA's Space Network. Since then, several astronauts have exercised this civic duty from orbit.

United States federal law states that national elections are to be held on the first Tuesday after the first Monday of November. It is a legal holiday in most states and in all territories. Many state elections are also held on this day. On Election Day, voters in each state and the District of Columbia mark a ballot for president and vice president. This balloting is called the *popular vote*. The popular vote does not directly decide the winner of the election. Instead, it determines the delegates who will represent each state and the District of Columbia in the Electoral College. These delegates officially elect the president and vice president.

Most elections are supervised on the local level by county election officials, who divide each county or ward into voting districts called *precincts*. Election officials determine the place where votes will be cast, called the *polling place* or the polls. They also check voters' names against registration lists, hand out ballots, and supervise the depositing of marked ballots in ballot boxes. In most states, the officials at each polling place must represent the two major political parties. In some areas, citizens' groups station observers called *poll watchers* at the polls to ensure that election officials perform their tasks honestly.

Voters indicate their choices privately in an enclosed voting booth. Many precincts use voting machines that automatically record votes. Every state allows citizens meeting certain requirements to vote by absentee ballot before the election.

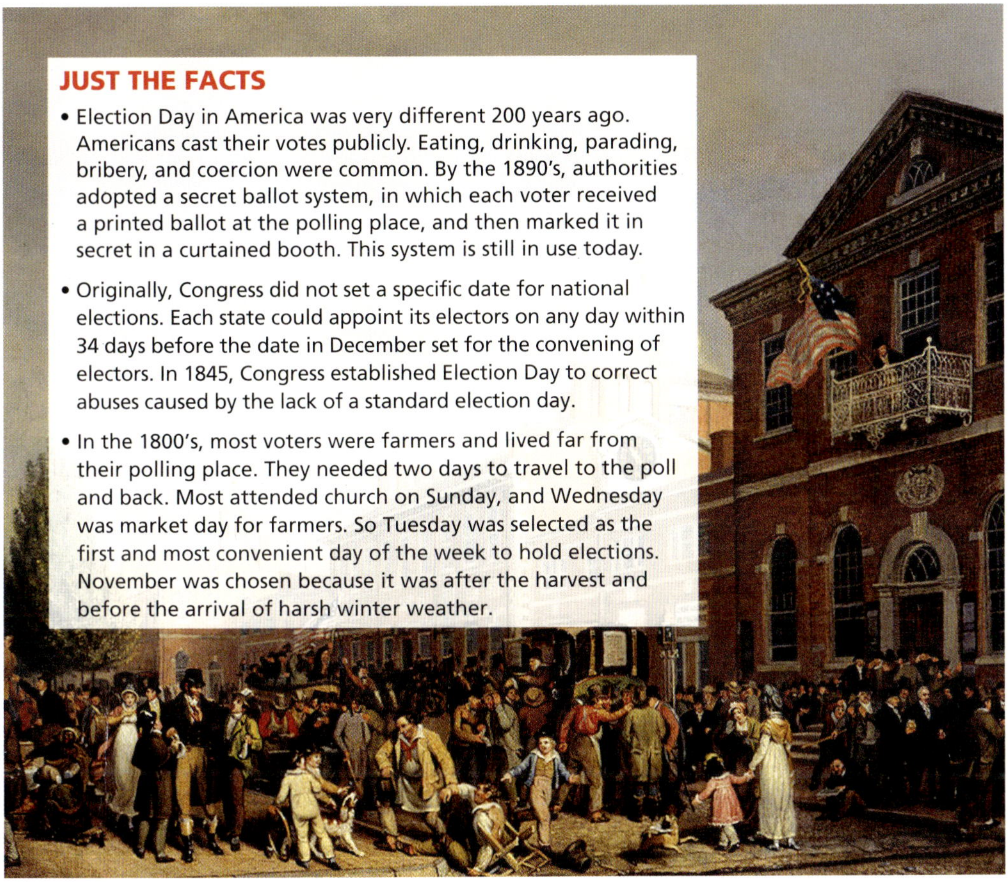

JUST THE FACTS

- Election Day in America was very different 200 years ago. Americans cast their votes publicly. Eating, drinking, parading, bribery, and coercion were common. By the 1890's, authorities adopted a secret ballot system, in which each voter received a printed ballot at the polling place, and then marked it in secret in a curtained booth. This system is still in use today.

- Originally, Congress did not set a specific date for national elections. Each state could appoint its electors on any day within 34 days before the date in December set for the convening of electors. In 1845, Congress established Election Day to correct abuses caused by the lack of a standard election day.

- In the 1800's, most voters were farmers and lived far from their polling place. They needed two days to travel to the poll and back. Most attended church on Sunday, and Wednesday was market day for farmers. So Tuesday was selected as the first and most convenient day of the week to hold elections. November was chosen because it was after the harvest and before the arrival of harsh winter weather.

The polls generally remain open from early morning until evening on Election Day. After the polls close, election officials count the votes for each candidate, including absentee votes. Then, all ballots and tally sheets from voting machines are sent, under seal, to city or county officials or to the board of elections. All state and national election results are filed with the chief election official, the secretary of state in most states. State and local officials then declare the winners in each race. Federal and state laws define dishonest voting practices and provide severe penalties for them. Such practices include bribing voters, impersonating another voter, stuffing a ballot box with forged votes, and tampering with voting machines. Laws also prohibit election officials from tampering with election results.

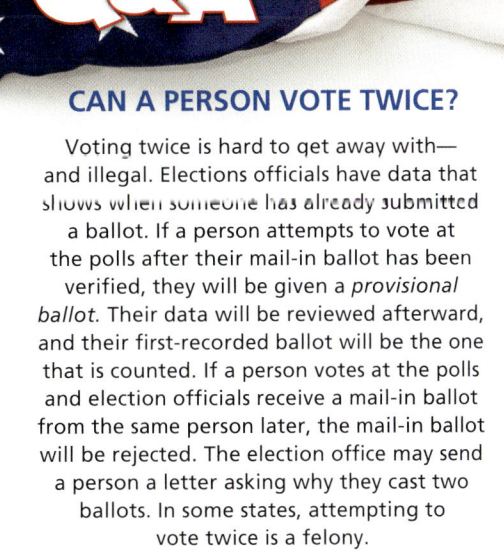

Q&A

CAN A PERSON VOTE TWICE?

Voting twice is hard to get away with—and illegal. Elections officials have data that shows when someone has already submitted a ballot. If a person attempts to vote at the polls after their mail-in ballot has been verified, they will be given a *provisional ballot*. Their data will be reviewed afterward, and their first-recorded ballot will be the one that is counted. If a person votes at the polls and election officials receive a mail-in ballot from the same person later, the mail-in ballot will be rejected. The election office may send a person a letter asking why they cast two ballots. In some states, attempting to vote twice is a felony.

TIME TO VOTE!

A Vietnamese immigrant celebrates with his family after becoming a naturalized citizen of the United States.

WHO IS QUALIFIED TO VOTE?

In most democracies, the only legal requirements for voting or for holding public office have to do with age, residence, and citizenship. The democratic process permits citizens to vote by secret ballot, free from force or bribes. It also requires that election results be protected against dishonesty.

To vote in national elections in the United States, Americans must:

Be a U.S. citizen. The U.S. Constitution grants citizenship to people born or *naturalized* in the United States. Naturalization is the legal process that allows foreign-born people to become a citizen in the country they have adopted.

Be at least 18 years of age.

Be registered to vote. *Registration* is the process by which a person's name is added to an official list of qualified voters. On election day, officials check each person's name against the registration list before they let the person vote. Voters can usually register in person or by mail. Registered voters receive a voter registration card. In most states, voters remain permanently registered unless they move.

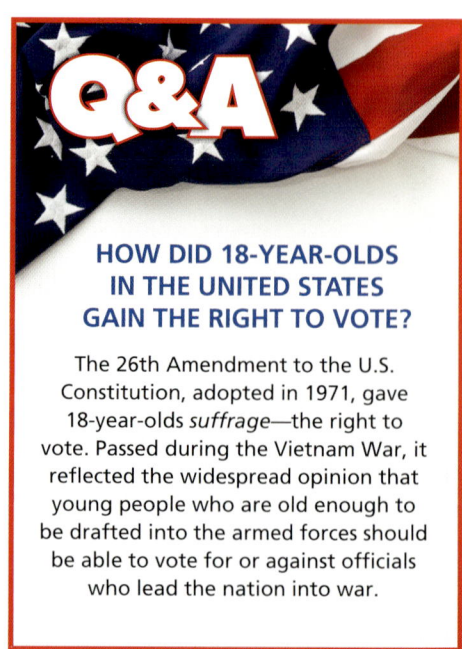

Q&A

HOW DID 18-YEAR-OLDS IN THE UNITED STATES GAIN THE RIGHT TO VOTE?

The 26th Amendment to the U.S. Constitution, adopted in 1971, gave 18-year-olds *suffrage*—the right to vote. Passed during the Vietnam War, it reflected the widespread opinion that young people who are old enough to be drafted into the armed forces should be able to vote for or against officials who lead the nation into war.

VOTING: A KEY FEATURE OF DEMOCRACY

The right of citizens to select their leaders is a key feature of *democracy,* a type of government ruled by the people. In fact, the word *democracy* means *rule by the people.* President Abraham Lincoln described such self-government as "government *of* the people, *by* the people, *for* the people."

Free elections give the people a chance to choose their leaders and express their opinions on issues. Elections are held periodically to ensure that elected officials truly represent the people. The possibility of being voted out of office helps assure that these officials pay attention to public opinion.

The United States government relies on the consent of the people. The government is a *representative democracy.* That means that the people elect representatives to act as their agents in making and enforcing laws. A healthy representative democracy depends on citizens exercising their right to vote. For this reason, many Americans consider voting not only a right, but a *civic duty*—that is, an important obligation or responsibility to their country—like serving on a jury or paying taxes.

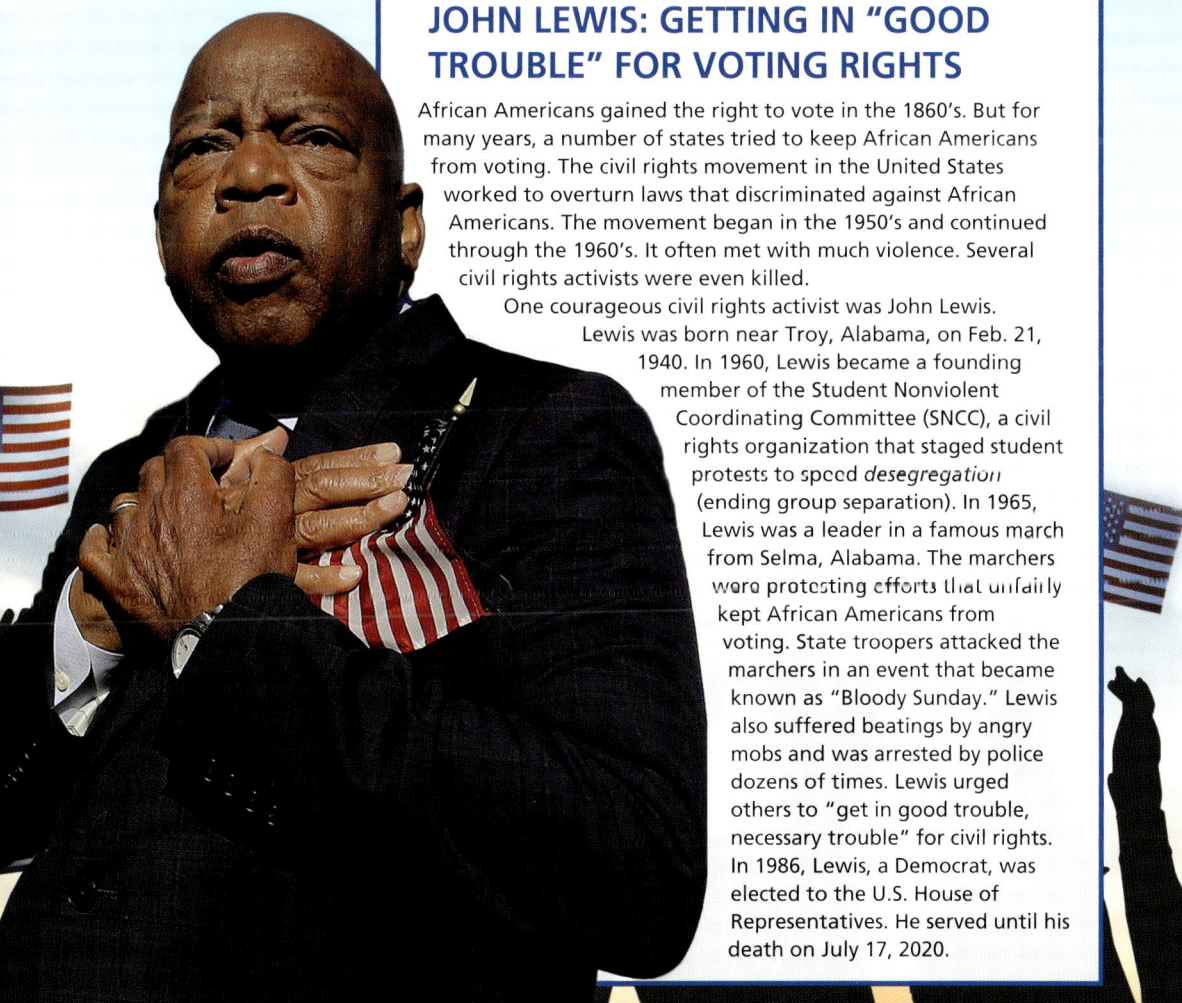

JOHN LEWIS: GETTING IN "GOOD TROUBLE" FOR VOTING RIGHTS

African Americans gained the right to vote in the 1860's. But for many years, a number of states tried to keep African Americans from voting. The civil rights movement in the United States worked to overturn laws that discriminated against African Americans. The movement began in the 1950's and continued through the 1960's. It often met with much violence. Several civil rights activists were even killed.

One courageous civil rights activist was John Lewis. Lewis was born near Troy, Alabama, on Feb. 21, 1940. In 1960, Lewis became a founding member of the Student Nonviolent Coordinating Committee (SNCC), a civil rights organization that staged student protests to speed *desegregation* (ending group separation). In 1965, Lewis was a leader in a famous march from Selma, Alabama. The marchers were protesting efforts that unfairly kept African Americans from voting. State troopers attacked the marchers in an event that became known as "Bloody Sunday." Lewis also suffered beatings by angry mobs and was arrested by police dozens of times. Lewis urged others to "get in good trouble, necessary trouble" for civil rights. In 1986, Lewis, a Democrat, was elected to the U.S. House of Representatives. He served until his death on July 17, 2020.

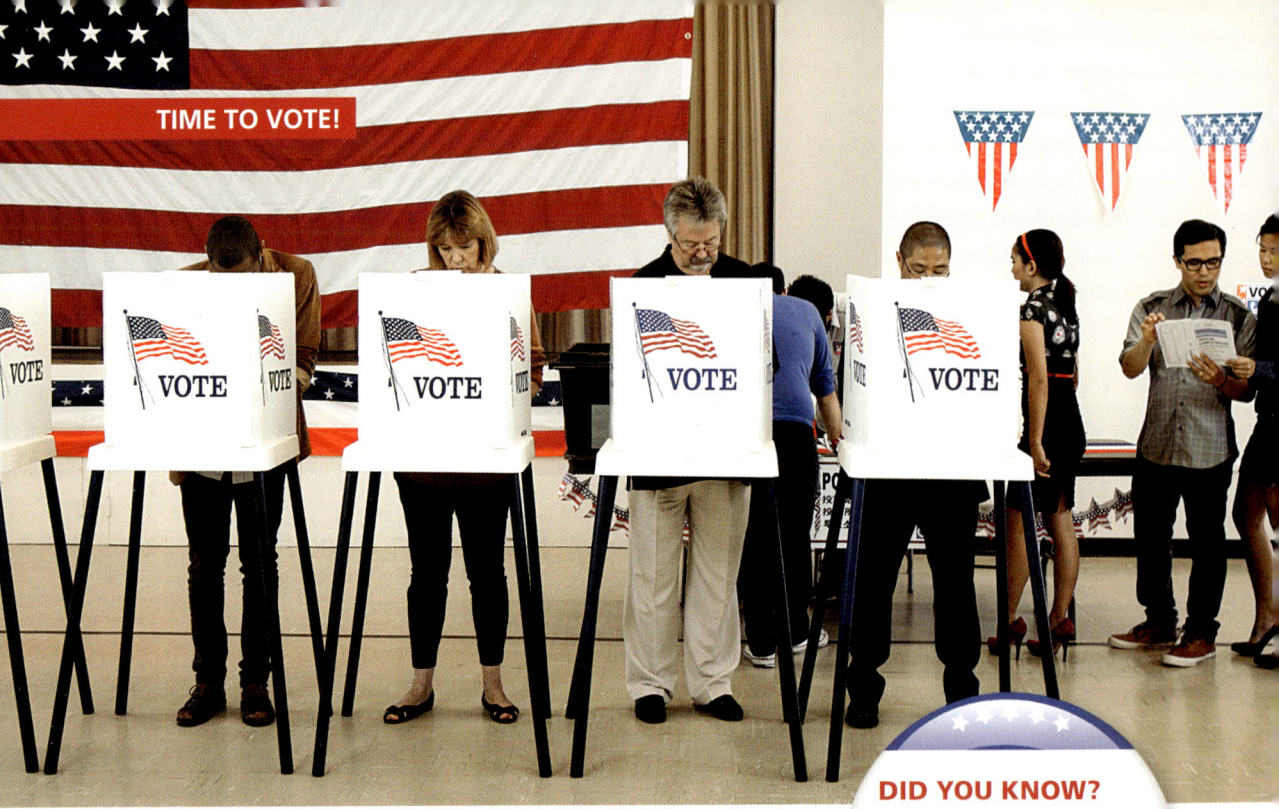

TIME TO VOTE!

DID YOU KNOW?
The word *ballot* comes from the French word *ballotte*, meaning a *little ball*. In ancient Athens, judges of the highest court gave their verdicts by dropping stone or metal balls into boxes.

CASTING YOUR BALLOT

Until the 1800's, voting was usually conducted orally and in public. Today, there are a number of ways to cast your ballot. Citizens may vote in person at a place called a *polling place,* or *poll,* while alone in a booth, or by mail.

Computerized voting machines became the most popular method of voting in the United States by the 1990's.

Punch card systems allow voters to select candidates by punching holes in computer cards. The cards are then fed into a card reader, and a computer totals all valid votes.

Optical scanning systems allow voters to mark ballots that are then fed into a computerized scanning device.

Other types of computerized systems allow voters to make selections by pushing buttons or by touching boxes on a computer screen.

Mail-in voting has become increasingly popular in the United States. In mail-in voting, a ballot is mailed to the home of a registered voter. The voter fills out the ballot and returns it by mail or drops it off in a secure drop box or voting center.

Absentee voting is a form of mail-in voting intended for citizens who are unable to vote in person. Absentee voters may include people in the armed forces, college students, people with disabilities, and travelers who are abroad on business or vacation.

Proxy vote allows a voter to authorize another person to cast a vote for him or her.

Early voting allows people to vote in special polling places before the election.

If a voting machine system is used, votes are counted automatically. But in some elections, paper ballots must be counted by hand. If the result of an election is close, one or more recounts may be held.

30

CASTING A BALLOT IN 2020

The 2020 presidential election set records for voter turnout. Some 160 million ballots were returned, and 67 percent of eligible voters cast ballots—the highest percentage since the election of 1900. Almost half of voters cast their ballot via mail—a process expanded in 2020 to more safely conduct the election during the COVID-19 pandemic. Of the voters who cast votes in person, half voted early and half cast votes on Election Day.

Absentee and other forms of mail-in voting traditionally have been embraced by voters of both parties. Military members posted overseas and retirees with second homes ranked among the practice's most common users. Voters used to have to provide a reason to vote by mail, but states began easing mail-in voting laws in the late 1900's. In such states as Colorado and Washington, vote-by-mail has been nearly universal since the early 2010's.

In 2020, fears of the coronavirus prompted officials in many states to expand voting by mail. President Donald J. Trump, however, became an outspoken opponent of the process and proclaimed it to be vulnerable to fraud.

Trump and his campaign associates encouraged Republican voters to vote in person. But tens of millions of voters of both parties cast absentee or mail-in ballots. Post-election polls showed that more than half of all voters for former Vice President Joe Biden—and about a third of Trump voters—cast ballots via mail. Trump voters were more than twice as likely as Biden voters to vote in person on November 3.

The counting of mail-in ballots varied widely by state. Florida law, for example, allowed election officials to sort and count mail-in ballots well before Election Day. In Pennsylvania and Wisconsin, state law prohibited the counting of such ballots until polls closed on November 3. Such rules delayed the certification of results for days after the election.

Trump's campaign filed more than 60 lawsuits challenging the constitutionality of state mail-in voting laws and demanding officials cease counting mail-in ballots. Campaign lawyers, however, failed to prove fraud charges in court to the judges' satisfaction. Late in November, Attorney General William Barr acknowledged that voting improprieties discovered to that time were not substantial enough to alter the outcome of the election.

JUST THE FACTS

Voting by mail has been a feature of every election since the Civil War (1861-1865). But in 2020, due to the COVID-19 pandemic, more Americans than ever before—almost half of all voters—cast a ballot by mail.

TIME TO VOTE!

JUST THE FACTS

Out of a population of about 334 million, about 160 million people in the United States voted in the 2020 presidential election. Only seven countries (besides the United States) have populations over 160 million: Bangladesh, Brazil, China, India, Indonesia, Nigeria, and Pakistan.

THE RESULTS OF THE 2020 ELECTION
POPULAR VOTE

JOE BIDEN
81,268,924

DONALD TRUMP
74,216,154

ELECTORAL COLLEGE

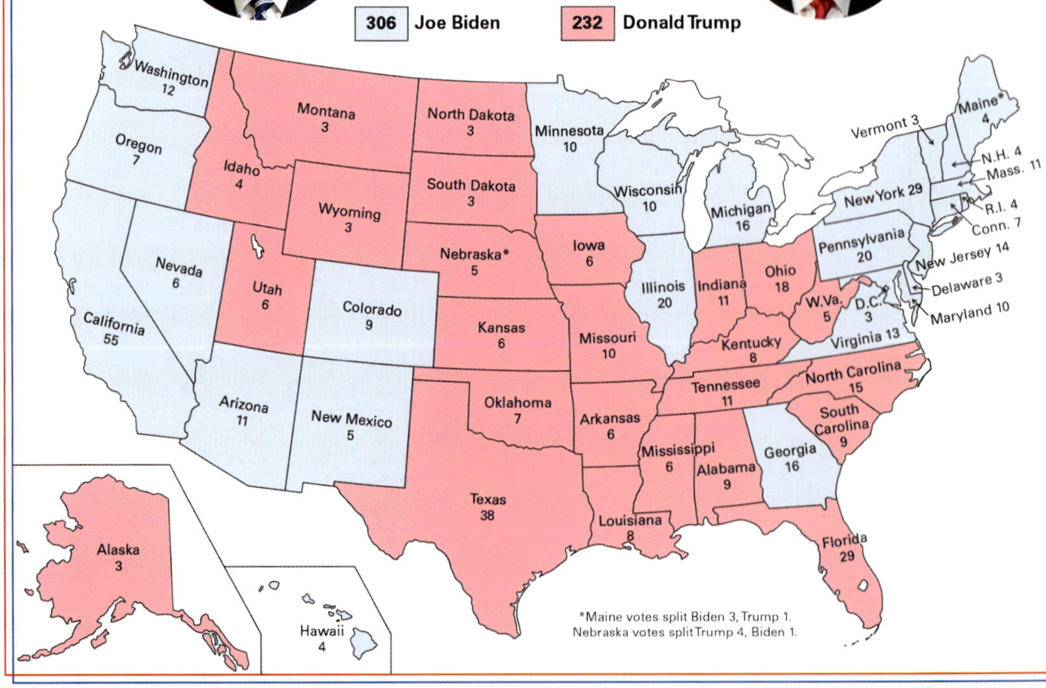

| 306 | Joe Biden | 232 | Donald Trump |

Washington 12
Montana 3
North Dakota 3
Minnesota 10
Maine 4
Oregon 7
Idaho 4
South Dakota 3
Wisconsin 10
Michigan 16
Vermont 3
N.H. 4
Mass. 11
New York 29
R.I. 4
Conn. 7
Wyoming 3
Nebraska* 5
Iowa 6
Ohio 18
Pennsylvania 20
New Jersey 14
Nevada 6
Utah 6
Colorado 9
Illinois 20
Indiana 11
W.Va. 5
D.C. 3
Delaware 3
Maryland 10
California 55
Kansas 6
Missouri 10
Kentucky 8
Virginia 13
Arizona 11
New Mexico 5
Oklahoma 7
Arkansas 6
Tennessee 11
North Carolina 15
South Carolina 9
Mississippi 6
Alabama 9
Georgia 16
Texas 38
Louisiana 8
Florida 29
Alaska 3
Hawaii 4

*Maine votes split Biden 3, Trump 1.
Nebraska votes split Trump 4, Biden 1.

POLL WATCHING AND POLL CHALLENGING

Poll watchers during the 2020 election had the special task of monitoring a record number of mail-in ballots. In addition, at many polling places, poll watchers were ordered to practice social distancing and stand 6 feet (2 meters) away from voters and election officials out of precaution because of the COVID-19 pandemic. Poll watchers are designated by a political party or campaign to ensure that election officials perform their tasks honestly. Poll watchers are not supposed to interfere in the electoral process, except to report issues to party officials or polling place authorities. A number of polling places were also observed by *poll challengers.* A poll challenger is someone who challenges whether a person is eligible to vote. Poll challengers may also be appointed by a political party, but they can only challenge eligibility based on actual knowledge, not an assumption. Both poll watchers and poll challengers may be known as partisan citizen observers, but the specific roles and terminology vary by state.

During the 2020 presidential election, the Trump campaign alleged that Republican poll watchers were being improperly denied access to observe the counting of ballots.

President Trump argued that there was a link between some of the complaints of partisan poll watchers—especially in key battleground states—and Joe Biden's win at the polls. Trump declared that in Pennsylvania, Democrats had gone to the state Supreme Court to ban Republican election observers. Lawyers for Trump's campaign filed a federal motion to stop the vote count in Philadelphia. However, after no evidence of Democrats attempting to ban Republican representatives from observing the counting of votes was found, the motion was denied. Trump also claimed that in Michigan, his campaign had been denied access to observe counting at the TCF Center in Detroit. However, election officials had prohibited all poll watchers at the center because the number of observers had reached the mandated capacity established because of the pandemic.

Both state and federal officials praised the 2020 election as safe and secure. In fact, the federal Cybersecurity and Infrastructure Security Agency (CISA) called the voting and count "the most secure in American history." CISA was established in 2018 when President Trump signed into law the Cybersecurity and Infrastructure Security Agency Act of 2018.

A poll watcher, *right,* monitors election workers hand-counting ballots during the 2020 presidential election.

Vice President Mike Pence presides over the Electoral College vote certification for President-elect Joe Biden, during a joint session of Congress at the U.S. Capitol on Jan. 6, 2021, in Washington, D.C.

HOW DOES THE PRESIDENT GET ELECTED?
THE ELECTORAL COLLEGE

The Electoral College is a group of representatives that formally elects the president and vice president of the United States. The Electoral College has 538 delegates, each of whom casts one electoral vote. To be elected president, a candidate must win a majority, or 270, of the electoral votes. Each state has as many electoral votes as the total of its representatives and senators in Congress. States with larger populations have more representatives, and therefore more electoral votes. The District of Columbia, which has no senators or representatives, has three electoral votes.

In December following the election, the electors in each state assemble and cast their ballots. After the electoral votes are cast, they are sent to the vice president of the United States, acting as president of the Senate, and to the head of the General Services Administration in Washington, D.C.

In January, at a joint session of Congress, the vice president opens and tallies the votes. One Democrat and one Republican from each chamber count the votes. The candidate who gets a majority of the electoral votes is declared elected. If no candidate has a majority, the state delegations in the House of Representatives

DID YOU KNOW?
Ronald Reagan received the greatest number of electoral votes of any president—525 in 1984.

choose the president from the three candidates with the highest number of electoral votes. In such an election, each state has one vote, determined by a majority vote among that state's delegation. If the vote is tied, the state is counted as abstaining.

Although the results are announced in January, the public usually finds out who the president will be a few hours after polls close on Election Day. This is because the popular vote in each state determines which candidate will win that state's electoral votes. In most states, the candidate who gets the most popular votes in a state will receive by custom or law all the state's electoral votes. In two states, Maine and Nebraska, the candidate who wins each congressional district receives the electoral vote for that district. Thus, the press can forecast the winner.

Some people argue that the Electoral College should be replaced with direct election of the president. They point out that the college has elected four presidents whose opponents received more popular votes: Rutherford B. Hayes in 1876, Benjamin Harrison in 1888, George W. Bush in 2000, and Donald J. Trump in 2016. Some people also argue that direct election might encourage third and fourth parties, and thus increase voter choice and voter turnout.

Other people believe the Electoral College system should be preserved. They argue that the direct election of the president would reduce the importance of individual states, particularly those with smaller populations. Without the Electoral College, candidates might be more likely to concentrate on highly populated states and ignore other parts of the country.

DID YOU KNOW?
There have been over 700 proposals introduced in Congress to reform or eliminate the Electoral College—more proposals than on any other subject.

Q&A

COULD THE U.S. SUPREME COURT DECIDE A PRESIDENTIAL ELECTION?

It can and it did—once. In December 2000, the Supreme Court settled the presidential election between Republican George W. Bush and Democrat Al Gore—one of the most unusual presidential elections in United States history.

On Nov. 7, 2000, over 100 million U.S. citizens voted. The race was extremely close between Texas Governor Bush and Vice President Gore. In Florida, the race was especially close. It became clear that the election depended on who won Florida's 25 electoral votes. The vote in Florida was so close that a recount of the votes was needed. After many disagreements, the Florida secretary of state declared on November 26 that Bush had won by 537 votes. But Gore asked that some votes be recounted by hand. The case went to the U.S. Supreme Court.

On December 12, the Supreme Court justices ruled that the Florida recounts should be stopped. In a televised address on December 13, Gore conceded the election to Bush. Gore, with 50,996,039 votes, received 48.38 percent of the popular vote. Bush received 50,456,141 votes and 47.87 percent of the popular vote. But Bush defeated Gore 271 to 266 in electoral votes, with one elector not casting a vote. In January 2001, George W. Bush became the nation's 43rd president.

A DARK DAY IN U.S. HISTORY

On the morning of Jan. 6, 2021, members of Congress convened at the U.S. Capitol to carry out the largely ceremonial task of certifying electoral votes. Vice President Mike Pence, as president of the Senate, presided over the count. However, the count was disrupted by protests that turned violent. Supporters of President Donald J. Trump, who had gathered to challenge the legitimacy of the election, stormed the Capitol, pushing through barriers and climbing walls. Lawmakers were quickly ushered to safety. Shouting and waving flags, the unruly mob entered the official chambers of Congress, as well as the personal offices of senators and representatives. Some damaged or stole property. Others took pictures of themselves occupying one of the nation's most sacred buildings. Violent protesters attacked U.S. Capitol police officers with metal pipes, chemical irritants, and other weapons. Several people were injured, and five people died, including a Capitol police officer who was struck in the head by a protester and killed, and a woman shot and killed by a Capitol police officer. Dozens of people were arrested after the attack, and hundreds were being investigated.

Several hours after the riot began, police and security officials cleared the Capitol. Lawmakers returned to the chambers to vote later that day, intent on certifying the election results. Joe Biden received 306 electoral votes, and Trump received 232. In the early morning hours of January 7, the United States certified its electoral count, making official Joe Biden's victory in the 2020 presidential election.

◀ Protesters scale the walls of the U.S. Capitol in Washington, D.C., on Jan. 6, 2021. Trump supporters stormed the building, intending to interrupt the Electoral College vote count certifying Joe Biden as president.

Protesters enter the ▶ official chambers of the U.S. Capitol on Jan. 6, 2021. Members of Congress took shelter as the unruly mob damaged or stole property.

THE SHOCK HEARD 'ROUND THE WORLD

World leaders expressed shock, and many called for peace after the Jan. 6, 2021, siege on the U.S. Capitol. Besides serving as a government office building, the Capitol is a symbol of the United States. Since its birth in 1776, the United States has been held up as the gold standard of freedom and democracy throughout the world. Some world leaders feared that the country's standing in the world might be diminished because of the attacks. Among U.S. adversaries, Russia and Iran said the attack showed the weakness of Western democracy. However, many U.S. allies believed democracy would prevail. Canadian Prime Minister Justin Trudeau said his people were "deeply disturbed and saddened by the attack on democracy in the United States.... Violence will never succeed in overruling the will of the people. Democracy in the U.S. must be upheld—and it will be."

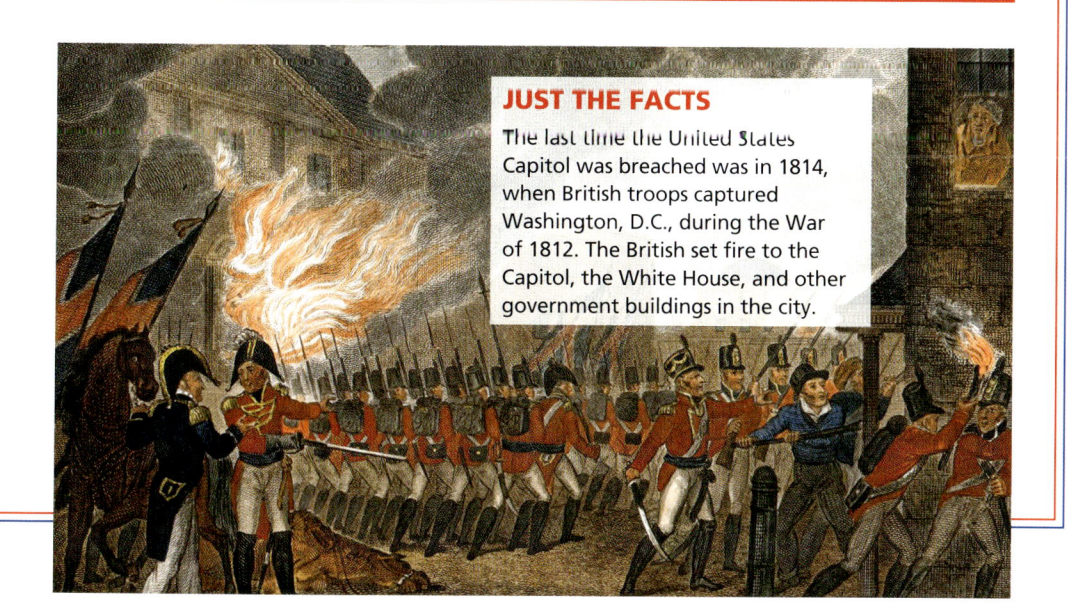

JUST THE FACTS

The last time the United States Capitol was breached was in 1814, when British troops captured Washington, D.C., during the War of 1812. The British set fire to the Capitol, the White House, and other government buildings in the city.

WHAT IS IMPEACHMENT?

Impeachment is the formal accusation of serious misconduct against a government official. The decision to accuse the official is brought by a vote of a legislative body. The impeached person may continue to perform the duties of office until he or she has been tried and found guilty of the charges.

It was at the Constitutional Convention in 1787 that, after much debate, the concept of impeachment of a U.S. president was approved. Among the debaters were George Washington, Alexander Hamilton, and Benjamin Franklin. Franklin favored impeachment but cited fairness, saying it would "be the best way therefore to provide in the Constitution for the regular punishment of the Executive, where his misconduct should deserve it, and for his honorable acquittal, where he should be unjustly accused." The impeachment process was included in Article II, Section 4 of the U.S. Constitution.

The U.S. House of Representatives uses its impeachment powers infrequently. The House has impeached only three presidents—Andrew Johnson, Bill Clinton, and Donald J. Trump (twice). In 1868, the House impeached Johnson, who had inherited a wartime dispute between his predecessor, President Abraham Lincoln, and Congress over how to treat

JUST THE FACTS
Richard Nixon was the only U.S. president to resign from office. He did so in 1974 to avoid impeachment for his involvement in the Watergate scandal.

the South after the Civil War. After impeachment, a Senate vote failed to remove Johnson from office. In 1998, the House of Representatives impeached Clinton for perjury and obstruction of justice. The charges developed out of Clinton's efforts to conceal an improper sexual relationship. The House sent its findings to the Senate, which conducted a trial and found Clinton not guilty. In late 2019, the House of Representatives impeached Trump for abusing his power as president by asking a foreign government—that of Ukraine—to investigate a political rival. The Senate acquitted Trump in early 2020. In January 2021, Trump was impeached again by the House of Representatives, this time for "inciting violence against the government of the United States." The accusation alleged that Trump encouraged supporters who stormed the U.S. Capitol. After an impeachment trial, which took place after Trump had left office, the Senate acquitted the former president.

DID YOU KNOW?
While presidential impeachments are rare in the United States, it is not unusual for members of Congress to introduce resolutions to remove a president from the office. Every president since Ronald Reagan (1981-1989) has been threatened at least once with impeachment by members of the House.

TWICE IMPEACHED, TWICE ACQUITTED

Trump's second impeachment trial took place in the Senate from February 9 to February 13, 2021. Seven Republican senators joined Democrats in voting to convict the former president on the charge of incitement of insurrection. The 57-to-43 vote fell 10 votes short, however, of the 67 votes required for a conviction. Mitch McConnell, the Republican leader in the Senate, said he believed it unconstitutional to impeach a former president and voted to acquit Trump. But he condemned the former president for inciting the Capitol riot. "There's no question, none, that President Trump is practically and morally responsible for provoking the events of the day," he said.

House impeachment managers proceed through the U.S. Capitol on Feb. 9, 2021, as the second impeachment trial of former President Donald Trump begins. Trump was acquitted on February 13.

President George W. Bush, *left*, and Vice President Richard B. Cheney

THE VICE PRESIDENT:

A HEARTBEAT AWAY

The vice president of the United States is only a heartbeat away from the most powerful elective office in the world. The vice president must be ready to become president or acting president at a moment's notice if the president dies, resigns, is removed from office, or becomes unable to perform the duties of office.

The U.S. Constitution gives the vice president no official duty other than that of presiding over the U.S. Senate as president of the Senate. The only vice presidential power is to break a tie vote in that body. For more than 100 years, the absence of political importance of the job caused it to be treated as somewhat of a joke. Even today, vice presidents who have assumed office on the death of a president are called "accidental presidents."

But the prestige of the vice presidency has gradually increased since the early 1920's, and today the office is as

DID YOU KNOW?

Richard B. Cheney has been cited as the most powerful vice president in American history. During the presidency of George W. Bush, Cheney had a substantial influence on many of the administration's major policy decisions. He served as a chief adviser to the president and was actively involved in decisions relating to national security, energy policy, and foreign affairs.

important as the president makes it. Some presidents have relied on the vice president's advice about party policy and political appointments. The vice president's participation in Cabinet meetings also depends on the wishes of the president.

The vice president makes numerous public appearances. One of the vice president's oldest responsibilities is that of ceremonial assistant to the president. In this capacity, the vice president greets visiting dignitaries at the airport and performs other ceremonial tasks.

The vice president's attendance at conferences between the president and congressional leaders strengthens the vice president's influence with the legislative branch. If the president gives the vice president important diplomatic missions, the vice president can help shape the foreign policy of the United States.

DID YOU KNOW?

Charles Curtis was the first biracial person to serve as vice president. Curtis was of Native American heritage. His mother was part Kaw (Kansa). He served as 31st vice president of the United States, under President Herbert Hoover, from 1929 to 1933. He had served in the U.S. House of Representatives from 1893 to 1907, and in the U.S. Senate from 1907 to 1913 and 1915 to 1929.

JUST THE FACTS

- The Founding Fathers originally provided that the person who received the second highest electoral vote for president should become vice president. Electors had two votes, which they cast for the two people they considered best qualified for the presidency.

- The rise of political parties caused the breakdown of the "runner-up" election system. In 1796, the Electoral College gave the greatest number of votes to John Adams, a Federalist. Thomas Jefferson, a Democratic-Republican, received the next largest number of votes, and became vice president. Adams and Jefferson became bitter rivals. The conflicting party loyalties of the two men created discord in the administration.

- In 1804, Congress adopted Amendment 12 to the Constitution, which provided for separate ballots for president and vice president. This solved the immediate problem, but it also lessened the prestige of the vice presidency. The vice president was no longer elected as the second choice for the presidency.

John Adams, *left*, and Thomas Jefferson

THE VICE PRESIDENT

"ACCIDENTAL PRESIDENTS"

Fifteen vice presidents have become president, eight because of the death of a president. These eight so-called "accidental presidents" were John Tyler, Millard Fillmore, Andrew Johnson, Chester A. Arthur, Theodore Roosevelt, Calvin Coolidge, Harry S. Truman, and Lyndon B. Johnson. The other vice presidents who became president were John Adams, Thomas Jefferson, Martin Van Buren, Richard M. Nixon, Gerald R. Ford, George H. W. Bush, and Joe Biden. Of these seven, all but Nixon and Biden became president immediately after serving as vice president. Ford was the only vice president to take office because of a president's resignation.

Lyndon B. Johnson takes the presidential oath of office aboard Air Force One on Nov. 22, 1963, after President John F. Kennedy was assassinated in Dallas. Johnson was the only president to take the oath of office aboard an airplane. He stands between his wife, Lady Bird Johnson, *left,* and Jacqueline Kennedy, the widow of the slain president.

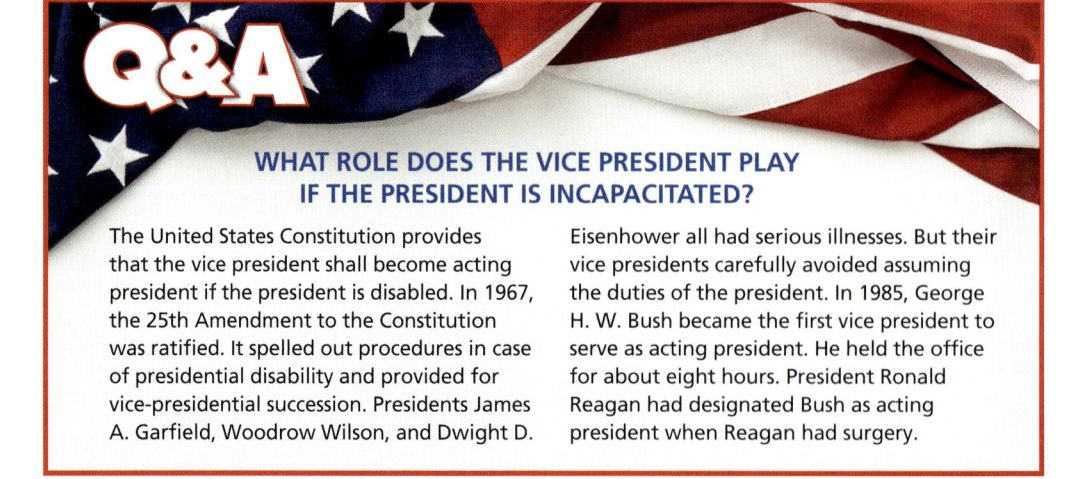

Q&A

WHAT ROLE DOES THE VICE PRESIDENT PLAY IF THE PRESIDENT IS INCAPACITATED?

The United States Constitution provides that the vice president shall become acting president if the president is disabled. In 1967, the 25th Amendment to the Constitution was ratified. It spelled out procedures in case of presidential disability and provided for vice-presidential succession. Presidents James A. Garfield, Woodrow Wilson, and Dwight D. Eisenhower all had serious illnesses. But their vice presidents carefully avoided assuming the duties of the president. In 1985, George H. W. Bush became the first vice president to serve as acting president. He held the office for about eight hours. President Ronald Reagan had designated Bush as acting president when Reagan had surgery.

PENCE REJECTS THE 25TH AMENDMENT

On the evening of Jan. 12, 2021, six days after a group of President Trump supporters stormed the U.S. Capitol, the House approved a resolution urging Vice President Mike Pence to invoke the 25th Amendment to the Constitution to remove Trump with a Cabinet vote. The resolution passed 223-205 almost entirely along party lines. It urged Pence to "declare what is obvious to a horrified Nation: That the President is unable to successfully discharge the duties and powers of his office." Hours before the vote, Pence sent a letter to House Speaker Nancy Pelosi, in which he said it would not be in the best interest of the nation to invoke the 25th Amendment, and that it was "time to unite our country as we prepare to inaugurate President-elect Joe Biden."

JUST THE FACTS

- In 1945, when First Lady Eleanor Roosevelt informed Vice President Harry S. Truman that her husband, Franklin D. Roosevelt, had died, Truman asked "Is there anything I can do for you?" Mrs. Roosevelt replied: "Is there anything we can do for you? For you are the one in trouble now." Truman felt unprepared to assume the presidency. "I felt like the moon, the stars, and all the planets had fallen on me," he said. Truman was left to deal with issues on which he'd never been briefed, including the atomic bomb, the potential of a Cold War, and the end of the war in the Pacific.

- President Dwight D. Eisenhower, who succeeded Truman in 1953, learned from his predecessor's unpreparedness. He gave his vice president, Richard Nixon, important duties and responsibilities. Eisenhower strengthened the vice presidency by directing that Nixon should preside at Cabinet meetings in the president's absence. Previously, the secretary of state had presided at such times. The next president, John F. Kennedy, also gave his vice president, Lyndon B. Johnson, important duties and responsibilities. When Kennedy was assassinated in 1963, many experts believed that Johnson was the best-prepared "accidental president."

Harry Truman, *left*, and Franklin D. Roosevelt

VICE PRESIDENT KAMALA HARRIS

In August 2020, with Joe Biden selecting Kamala Harris as his vice-presidential running mate, Harris became the first Black woman and the first person of Indian descent to be placed on the presidential ticket of a major political party. In January 2021, after taking the oath of office, Harris became the United States' first female vice president and the first African American and Asian American vice president.

Justice Sonia Sotomayor, the first Hispanic American to serve on the Supreme Court, administered the swearing in of Harris in front of the U.S. Capitol on Inauguration Day. That evening, in her first speech as vice president of the United States, Harris said of Americans, "We not only dream, we do. We not only see what has been, we see what can be. We shoot for the moon and then we plant our flag on it. We are bold, fearless, and ambitious. We are undaunted in our belief that we shall overcome, that we will rise up."

Before becoming vice president, Harris represented California in the U.S. Senate since 2017. She had earlier served as California's attorney general—the state's chief law officer. Prior to serving as attorney general, Harris was the district attorney of San Francisco, California.

Kamala Devi Harris was born in Oakland, California, on Oct. 20, 1964. Her mother was a physician and cancer specialist who was born in India. Her father, who was born in Jamaica, became an economics professor. In 1986, Harris received a bachelor's degree in political science and economics from Howard University. In 1989, she earned a law degree from the University of California's Hastings College of the Law in San Francisco. Harris married Doug Emhoff, an entertainment lawyer, in 2014.

Kamala Harris takes the vice presidential oath of office on Jan. 20, 2021. Her husband, Second Gentleman Doug Emhoff, stands next to her.

From 1990 to 1998, Harris served as deputy district attorney for Alameda County, California. In 1998, she became the managing attorney of the Career Criminal Unit of the San Francisco District Attorney's Office. In 2000, she was named to lead the San Francisco City Attorney's Division on Families and Children.

In 2003, Harris won election as San Francisco district attorney. She was reelected in 2007 and served through 2010. Her victory in the 2010 campaign for state attorney general marked the first time that a woman and—because of her mixed ethnicity—a person of African American and South Asian ancestry won the post. Harris took office in 2011. As attorney general, she gained attention for her work to combat transnational gangs and investigate banks that engaged in mortgage fraud. She was reelected in 2014 and served until 2017.

In January 2015, Barbara Boxer, long-time U.S. senator from California, announced that she would not seek reelection in 2016. Shortly afterward, Harris announced that she would campaign for the open Senate seat. In June 2016, Harris finished first in California's open primary for the U.S. Senate seat. She defeated U.S. Congresswoman Loretta Sanchez, a fellow Democrat, in the November election. As a U.S. senator, Harris served on a number of committees, including the Judiciary Committee and the Select Committee on Intelligence.

In January 2019, Harris began a campaign for her party's 2020 nomination for president. She dropped out of the race in December 2019, while trailing her competitors in fundraising and public opinion poll support. Also in 2019, Harris published a memoir, *The Truths We Hold: An American Journey*.

DID YOU KNOW?
Geraldine Ferraro was the first woman chosen as a vice presidential candidate by a major American political party. Ferraro, a Democrat, and her presidential running mate, former Vice President Walter F. Mondale, were defeated by their Republican opponents, President Ronald Reagan and Vice President George H. W. Bush. Ferraro had served three terms in the United States House of Representatives.

BREAKING THE TIE

The 117th United States Congress convened on Jan. 3, 2021. On January 5, Georgia held two runoff elections for the U.S. Senate, as no candidate received a majority of votes in either the regularly scheduled election or the special election on Nov. 3, 2020. Democrat Raphael Warnock defeated Republican Kelly Loeffler in the special runoff election. Democrat Jon Ossoff defeated Republican David Perdue in the regular runoff election. This left both parties with 50 Senate seats.

On Jan. 18, 2021, Kamala Harris officially resigned her U.S. Senate seat, ending her four-year Senate career. California Governor Gavin Newsom named former California Secretary of State Alex Padilla, a Democrat, to fill Harris's seat. On Inauguration Day, January 20, Harris was sworn in as vice president. In her new role as president of the Senate, Harris will cast the tie-breaking vote in that chamber, giving the Democrats slim control. The vote shifts the balance of power in Congress, as Democrats now control both chambers. Chuck Schumer of New York became Senate majority leader. California Representative Nancy Pelosi retained her seat as speaker of the House.

JUST THE FACTS
Kamala Harris is the daughter of immigrants. Her Indian mother left her with a motto that she lives by: "You may be the first, but make sure you're not the last."

Kamala Harris, *right*, and her mother, Shyamala Gopalan.

Barack Obama, *left,* and Donald Trump, in 2016

PRESIDENTIAL TRANSITION

The presidential transition occurs in a roughly 11-week period between Election Day, in early November, and Inauguration Day, on January 20. Some of the elements of the process are codified by law, while others stand as part of a time-honored tradition. Throughout U.S. history, outgoing administrations have utilized the transition period to brief their successors on key domestic and national security issues. The president-elect utilizes this time to nominate Cabinet officials, propose candidates for other key roles that require confirmation by the Senate, and enact succession plans for a host of federal agencies. The Office of Management and Budget and the General Services Administration maintain much of the responsibility for transition matters.

In 1963, Congress passed the Presidential Transition Act to establish guidelines for the federal government to prepare for an orderly transfer of power between administrations. Transition matters had earlier been covered by a combination of laws and traditions. Provisions of the act, which has been updated several times since its original passage, allow some transition planning to occur among eligible candidates prior to an election.

DID YOU KNOW?
The 20th Amendment, known as the Lame Duck Amendment, changed the inauguration date from March 4 to January 20. It also moved, from March 4 to January 3, the opening date of the new Congress. The amendment abridged the time in which losing candidates could continue to influence lawmaking. It also prevented outgoing U.S. representatives from choosing a president should no candidate receive a majority in the Electoral College.

ELECTION 2020: A DISORDERLY TRANSITION

President Trump's campaign lost a series of legal challenges in the weeks after the election. On Nov. 23, 2020, following the certification of Joe Biden's victories in several states that conducted recounts, the General Services Administration (GSA) formally authorized the start of the transition to a Biden administration. The authorization allowed Biden's transition team to utilize funds provided by the Presidential Transition Act and begin communicating with federal agencies. Biden announced nominations for several Cabinet positions and notably appointed infectious disease expert Dr. Anthony Fauci to lead his COVID-19 response team. In December, Biden expressed frustration that officials at the Department of Defense had provided only limited national security briefings. Defense officials claimed, however, that they had cooperated in earnest. Some observers attributed the flawed transition to Trump's dismissal of Defense Secretary Mark Esper following the election. Handoff activities among other agencies proceeded more smoothly.

Despite the GSA's formal sign-off on the transition, the president did not accept election defeat and repeatedly vowed never to concede to Biden. On Jan. 7, 2021, a day after the violent siege of the U.S. Capitol, Trump pledged a "smooth, orderly, and seamless transition of power." Presidential historians said that the delay in the GSA's electoral certification, together with Trump's unceasing claims of a rigged election, had served to delay confirmation of Biden's nominees for weeks or months. Nominees for key national security posts—including the secretaries of defense, state, and homeland security—are customarily granted Senate confirmation hearings prior to or soon after an inauguration.

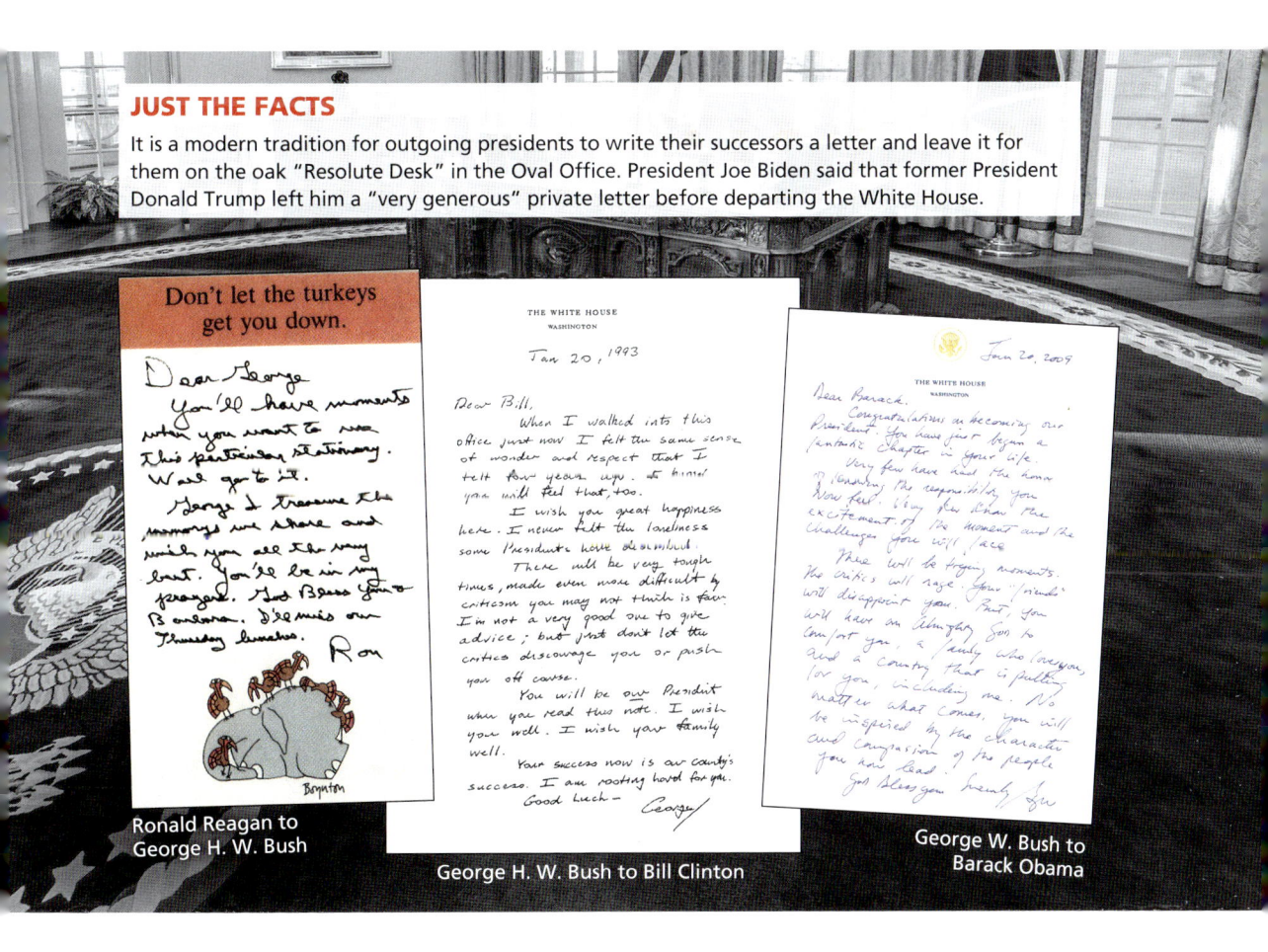

JUST THE FACTS

It is a modern tradition for outgoing presidents to write their successors a letter and leave it for them on the oak "Resolute Desk" in the Oval Office. President Joe Biden said that former President Donald Trump left him a "very generous" private letter before departing the White House.

Ronald Reagan to George H. W. Bush

George H. W. Bush to Bill Clinton

George W. Bush to Barack Obama

INAUGURATION DAY

The inauguration is the ceremony of installing the newly elected or reelected president in office. It is held at noon on January 20 after the election. Hundreds of thousands of spectators attend the inauguration, which usually takes place outside the U.S. Capitol in Washington, D.C. Millions of other Americans watch the event on television.

The highlight of the inauguration ceremony occurs when the newly elected or reelected president takes the oath of office from the chief justice of the Supreme Court. With right hand raised and left hand on a Bible, the newly elected or reelected president says: "I do solemnly swear (or affirm) that I will faithfully execute the office of president of the United States, and will to the best of my ability, preserve, protect and defend the Constitution of the United States."

Soon after being sworn in, the president and vice president, accompanied by their spouses, traditionally lead a patriotic parade from the Capitol to 1600 Pennsylvania Avenue, the address of the White House, the president's official residence. During past inaugurations, lively inaugural balls have been held throughout the city. At each one, a band would play "Hail to the Chief" for the president and "Hail Columbia" for the vice president. The new term for the elected president then begins.

Joe Biden is sworn in as the 46th president of the United States on Jan. 20, 2021. His wife, Jill Biden, holds a family heirloom Bible.

DID YOU KNOW?

The location of the inauguration was moved from the east side of the Capitol to the west side by the Joint Committee on the Inauguration. The decision was made to save money and provide more space for spectators. Ronald Reagan's inauguration in 1981 was the first to take advantage of the striking vista overlooking the National Mall, with its iconic Washington Monument and distant Lincoln Memorial.

JUST THE FACTS

- George Washington's first inauguration, in 1789, was held in New York City; his second, in 1793, was held in Philadelphia.

- Washington's second inaugural address was the shortest: 135 words.

- The inaugural parade is a tradition that dates back to 1801, when Thomas Jefferson rode a horse from Congress's house to the president's house after his swearing in. He was the first president to be inaugurated in Washington, D.C.

- The first first lady to take part in her husband's inaugural ceremony was Lady Bird Johnson, in 1965. She held the Bible while Lyndon B. Johnson took the oath of office.

- William Henry Harrison served the shortest time in office of any president in American history. He caught a cold the day he was inaugurated president, on March 4, 1841, and died 30 days later, on April 4. Harrison was the first president to die in office.

- In 1933, the 20th Amendment made the inauguration a midwinter event when it changed the date from March 4 to January 20. Franklin D. Roosevelt was the first President sworn in on the new date.

- Ronald Reagan's two inaugurations were the hottest and coldest. His first, on Jan. 20, 1981, was the warmest, at 55 °F; his second, on Jan. 21, 1985, was the coldest, at 7 °F. (January 20 fell on a Sunday, so Reagan was privately sworn in that day at the White House; the public inauguration on January 21 took place in the Capitol Rotunda, due to the freezing weather.)

- Barack Obama was sworn in four times. During his first inauguration in 2009, Chief Justice John Roberts misstated a few words while administering the oath of office. Obama was sworn in again the next day "out of an abundance of caution." He was sworn in for his second term in 2013. Because January 20 fell on a Sunday, he took the oath privately that day, then publicly the next day. The only other president who was sworn in four times was Franklin D. Roosevelt, who served four terms.

The inauguration of President Barack Obama, 2008

INAUGURATION DAY

Former President Lyndon B. Johnson, *left,* shakes hands with newly inaugurated Richard M. Nixon in 1969. Outgoing presidents usually attend the inauguration of their successor.

Q&A

WHICH PRESIDENTS DID NOT ATTEND THEIR SUCCESSOR'S INAUGURATION?

While most outgoing presidents have appeared on the inaugural platform with their successor, they are not required to, and several did not:

- John Adams, grieving his defeat to his rival Thomas Jefferson and the death of his son Charles, refused to stay in Washington, D.C., for Jefferson's inauguration. He hurried off for his home in Quincy, Massachusetts, on the morning of March 4, 1801.

- Adams's son John Quincy Adams also left Washington, D.C., skipping the 1829 inauguration of Andrew Jackson.

- Martin Van Buren, for reasons unknown, did not attend the 1841 inauguration of William Henry Harrison.

- Andrew Johnson, the first president to be impeached, conducted a final cabinet meeting rather than attend the 1869 inauguration of Ulysses S. Grant.

- Donald J. Trump held a "departure ceremony" and then left Washington, D.C., for his Mar-A-Lago estate in Palm Beach, Florida, prior to the 2021 inauguration of Joe Biden.

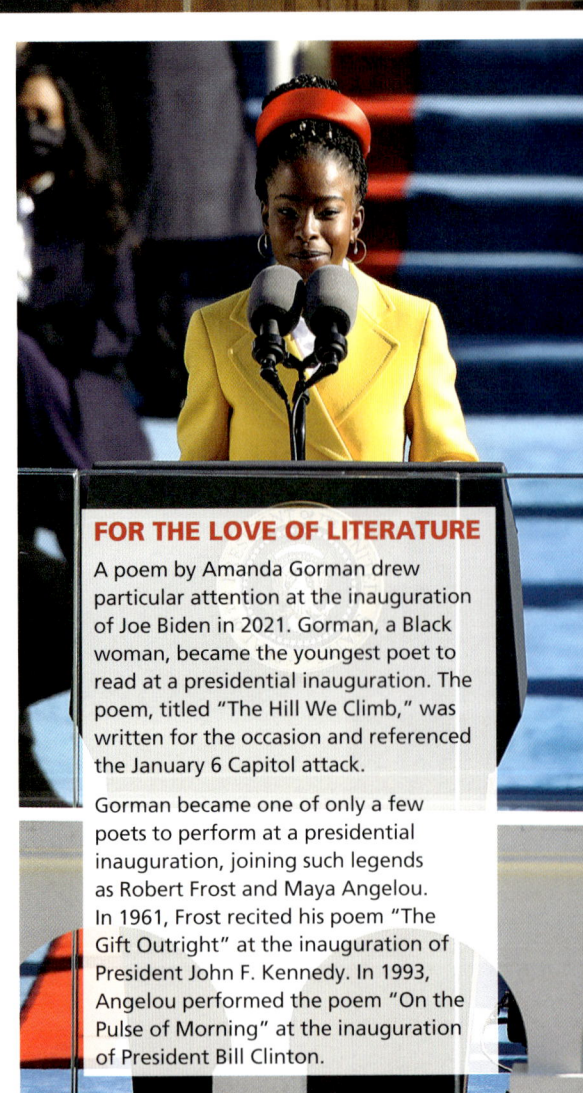

FOR THE LOVE OF LITERATURE

A poem by Amanda Gorman drew particular attention at the inauguration of Joe Biden in 2021. Gorman, a Black woman, became the youngest poet to read at a presidential inauguration. The poem, titled "The Hill We Climb," was written for the occasion and referenced the January 6 Capitol attack.

Gorman became one of only a few poets to perform at a presidential inauguration, joining such legends as Robert Frost and Maya Angelou. In 1961, Frost recited his poem "The Gift Outright" at the inauguration of President John F. Kennedy. In 1993, Angelou performed the poem "On the Pulse of Morning" at the inauguration of President Bill Clinton.

A DIFFERENT KIND OF INAUGURATION

Joe Biden became the 46th president of the United States on Jan. 20, 2021. His inauguration looked different than inaugurations past. Because of the ongoing COVID-19 pandemic, efforts were made to limit the size of crowds and prevent the spread of the virus. Gone were the parades and balls. Instead, the country marked the transition of power with virtual parades and televised performances.

As is tradition, the chief justice of the Supreme Court of the United States swore in the incoming president. In 2021, that honor went to Chief Justice John G. Roberts, Jr. Biden then gave his inaugural address and conducted a review of military troops. Celebrities were on hand to help celebrate the occasion. Lady Gaga performed the national anthem, and Jennifer Lopez and Garth Brooks gave musical performances.

The events took place on the west front of the United States Capitol—which, only two weeks before, had been stormed by protesters intent on halting Biden's certification as winner of the presidential election. President Donald Trump did not attend the inauguration ceremony, becoming one of only a handful of outgoing presidents to skip the inauguration.

Thousands of military troops and police officers were stationed at the Capitol—and at state capitols around the country—in anticipation of further violence. Experts had warned of far-right extremist groups' desire to stage attacks at such locations on or around Inauguration Day. In the weeks leading up to the inauguration, 15,000 troops—more soldiers than the United States had in Iraq and Afghanistan at that time—had been stationed in Washington, D.C. The weekend before the inauguration, several groups of armed protesters showed up at the capitols of such states as Michigan, Ohio, and Texas. They were met with military vehicles and police barricades.

Another major threat to the United States—COVID-19—led officials to scale down inauguration celebrations. Biden's inauguration schedule began the evening before Inauguration Day, with a somber memorial to the 400,000 Americans who had to that date died from the disease, held at the Lincoln Memorial Reflecting Pool on the National Mall.

To limit the spread of the virus, tickets for the events were not made available to the general public. And instead of a traditional parade down Pennsylvania Avenue, there was a virtual parade featuring music, poetry, and dance. The parade honored America's *frontline workers* (workers likely to encounter COVID-19). In place of balls in honor of the new president, there was a star-studded television event called "Celebrating America" on the evening of the inauguration. Hosted by actor Tom Hanks, the event featured such musicians and actors as Demi Lovato, Justin Timberlake, and Kerry Washington. The television event ended a day filled with celebration and patriotism.

U.S. National Guard troops take position outside the U.S. Capitol as the inauguration of President-elect Joe Biden begins on Jan. 20, 2021.

Former President Jimmy Carter, *center*, takes part in a Habitat for Humanity project in Washington, D.C., in October 2010.

PRESIDENTIAL LEGACY

Many presidents remained active in public service after leaving the White House. Some continued to work in government. John Quincy Adams, a former U.S. senator, was elected to the U.S. House of Representatives in 1830, shortly after he failed to win a second term as president. He was the only former president elected to the House. Adams served in the House for 17 years. Andrew Johnson won election to the U.S. Senate in 1875, and thus became the only former president to serve as a senator. In 1921, President Warren G. Harding appointed William Howard Taft chief justice of the Supreme Court. Taft was the only former president to serve as chief justice.

Every president since Calvin Coolidge has published a memoir after leaving office. Ulysses S. Grant's *Personal Memoirs* (1885), which covers his life up through the end of the American Civil War (1861-1865), is considered by historians to be among the best by a U.S. president. Many books written by former presidents have become bestsellers. Many former presidents have also had successful and lucrative speaking careers after leaving office.

Several former presidents became active in humanitarian projects. Since the mid-1980's, Jimmy Carter has worked as a volunteer carpenter on projects for Habitat for Humanity, a nonprofit organization that builds houses for the poor. Carter won the Nobel Peace Prize in 2002 for working to find peaceful solutions to international conflicts. In 2005, President George W. Bush appointed Bill Clinton and Bush's father, former President George H. W. Bush, to head efforts to raise money for global tsunami and hurricane disaster relief. In 2010, President Barack Obama also involved Clinton in disaster relief. Clinton joined with George W. Bush to lead a fund-raising effort to aid earthquake victims.

PRESIDENTIAL LIBRARIES

One of a former president's most important legacies is the establishment of a presidential library. Presidential libraries collect papers, records, and other items associated with a former United States president. Many people visit a presidential library to study its books, newspapers, films, photographs, sound and video recordings, and other documents. A presidential library also includes a museum with exhibits that tell the story of the life and career of the president.

DID YOU KNOW?
The presidential library system formally began in 1939, when President Franklin D. Roosevelt donated his personal and presidential papers to the federal government. The Presidential Libraries Act of 1955 was set up to encourage presidents to donate their historical materials to the government. It ensures the preservation of presidential papers and their availability to the American people.

The National Archives and Records Administration (NARA) administers 13 presidential libraries (see below). Other presidential libraries and museums are not managed by NARA. For example, the Illinois Historic Preservation Agency, a state government agency, administers the Abraham Lincoln Presidential Library and Museum in Springfield, Illinois. The Rutherford B. Hayes Presidential Center in Fremont, Ohio, is a private, nonprofit institution that includes a library and museum. The Forbes Library, a public library in Northampton, Massachusetts, houses the Calvin Coolidge Presidential Library and Museum. The William McKinley Presidential Library and Museum in Canton, Ohio, and the Woodrow Wilson Presidential Library and Museum in Staunton, Virginia, are both private, nonprofit institutions.

In 2015, the University of Chicago, where President Barack Obama once taught law, was chosen to host the Obama Presidential Center. The center is to be built on parkland on Chicago's South Side near the university campus and will feature a library, a museum, and other facilities.

Q&A

WHERE ARE SOME PRESIDENTIAL LIBRARIES?

NARA manages the following presidential libraries:

George Bush Library and Museum	College Station, Texas
George W. Bush Library and Museum	Dallas, Texas
Jimmy Carter Library and Museum	Atlanta, Georgia
William J. Clinton Library and Museum	Little Rock, Arkansas
Dwight D. Eisenhower Library, Museum, and Boyhood Home	Abilene, Kansas
Gerald R. Ford Library and Museum	Ann Arbor and Grand Rapids, Michigan
Herbert Hoover Library and Museum	West Branch, Iowa
Lyndon Baines Johnson Library and Museum	Austin, Texas
John F. Kennedy Library and Museum	Boston, Massachusetts
Richard Nixon Library and Museum	Yorba Linda, California
Ronald Reagan Library and Museum	Simi Valley, California
Franklin D. Roosevelt Library and Museum	Hyde Park, New York
Harry S. Truman Library and Museum	Independence, Missouri

HAIL TO THE CHIEF

There have been 46 presidents of the United States since 1789. What have you learned about them? Test your knowledge with the quiz on the next page.

1. George Washington	(1789-1797)	unaffiliated
2. John Adams	(1797-1801)	Federalist
3. Thomas Jefferson	(1801-1809)	Democratic-Republican
4. James Madison	(1809-1817)	Democratic-Republican
5. James Monroe	(1817-1825)	Democratic-Republican
6. John Quincy Adams	(1825-1829)	Democratic-Republican/ National Republican[1]
7. Andrew Jackson	(1829-1837)	Democratic
8. Martin Van Buren	(1837-1841)	Democratic
9. William H. Harrison	(1841)	Whig
10. John Tyler	(1841-1845)	Whig
11. James K. Polk	(1845-1849)	Democratic
12. Zachary Taylor	(1849-1850)	Whig
13. Millard Fillmore	(1850-1853)	Whig
14. Franklin Pierce	(1853-1857)	Democratic
15. James Buchanan	(1857-1861)	Democratic
16. Abraham Lincoln	(1861-1865)	Republican, Union[2]
17. Andrew Johnson	(1865-1869)	Union[3]
18. Ulysses S. Grant	(1869-1877)	Republican
19. Rutherford B. Hayes	(1877-1881)	Republican
20. James A. Garfield	(1881)	Republican
21. Chester A. Arthur	(1881-1885)	Republican
22. Grover Cleveland	(1885-1889)	Democratic
23. Benjamin Harrison	(1889-1893)	Republican
24. Grover Cleveland	(1893-1897)	Democratic
25. William McKinley	(1897-1901)	Republican
26. Theodore Roosevelt	(1901-1909)	Republican
27. William H. Taft	(1909-1913)	Republican
28. Woodrow Wilson	(1913-1921)	Democratic
29. Warren G. Harding	(1921-1923)	Republican
30. Calvin Coolidge	(1923-1929)	Republican
31. Herbert Hoover	(1929-1933)	Republican
32. Franklin D. Roosevelt	(1933-1945)	Democratic
33. Harry S. Truman	(1945-1953)	Democratic
34. Dwight D. Eisenhower	(1953-1961)	Republican
35. John F. Kennedy	(1961-1963)	Democratic
36. Lyndon B. Johnson	(1963-1969)	Democratic
37. Richard M. Nixon	(1969-1974)	Republican
38. Gerald R. Ford	(1974-1977)	Republican
39. Jimmy Carter	(1977-1981)	Democratic
40. Ronald W. Reagan	(1981-1989)	Republican
41. George H. W. Bush	(1989-1993)	Republican
42. Bill Clinton	(1993-2001)	Democratic
43. George Walker Bush	(2001-2009)	Republican
44. Barack Obama	(2009-2017)	Democratic
45. Donald J. Trump	(2017-2021)	Republican
46. Joe Biden	(2021-)	Democratic

[1] The Democratic-Republican Party split soon after the 1824 election. John Quincy Adams's supporters became known as the National Republicans.
[2] The Union Party consisted of Republicans and War Democrats.
[3] The Union Party consisted of Republicans and War Democrats; Johnson was a War Democrat.

George Washington

WHAT DID YOU LEARN ABOUT THE PRESIDENTS?

1. Who was the only president who did not belong to a political party?
2. Who was the only president who did not win election to either the office of vice president or the office of president?
3. Who was the only president to serve two nonconsecutive terms?
4. Which president was sworn into office on an airplane?
5. Who was the only former president to serve as chief justice of the Supreme Court of the United States?
6. Who were the only former vice presidents who became president but did not succeed the president under whom they served?
7. Who was the first president to hold a televised press conference?
8. Which president served the shortest time in office?
9. Which president served the longest?
10. Which president received the greatest number of electoral votes?
11. Which four presidents were elected by the Electoral College, even though their opponents received more popular votes?
12. Who was the only president to resign?
13. Who was the youngest person ever to become president?
14. Who was the youngest person ever elected president?
15. Who was the oldest person ever elected president?
16. Which presidents have been impeached?
17. Who was the only president to be impeached twice?
18. Which president won the Nobel Peace Prize after leaving office?
19. Who were the only presidents elected to Congress after leaving office?
20. Who was the only president who was elected unanimously?
21. Who was the first president to be inaugurated in Washington, D.C.?
22. Who was the first president to die in office?
23. Who was the first president to be sworn in on January 20?
24. Who became president as a result of a U.S. Supreme Court decision?
25. Which president was the first "dark horse" candidate?
26. Which two presidents were sworn in four times?
27. Which two presidents were elected by the U.S. House of Representatives?
28. Which president later ran as a candidate for the first Progressive Party?
29. Which two presidential candidates—who both later became president—were the first to debate on television?
30. Which two candidates went on to win the presidency after losing both the Iowa caucus and the New Hampshire primary?

The answers are on page 64.

Ulysses S. Grant

William McKinley

James K. Polk

DID YOU KNOW?
"Hail to the Chief" is the personal anthem of the president of the United States. Based on an old Scottish melody, it achieved its status as a ceremonial tribute to the president when Sarah Childress Polk had it played at the inauguration of her husband, James K. Polk, in 1845.

Donald J. Trump

Benjamin Harrison

**FROM THE PAGES
OF THE 2022 EDITION OF
*THE WORLD BOOK ENCYCLOPEDIA***

**46th president of the
United States 2021-**

Trump
45th president
2017-2021
Republican

Biden
46th president
2021-
Democrat

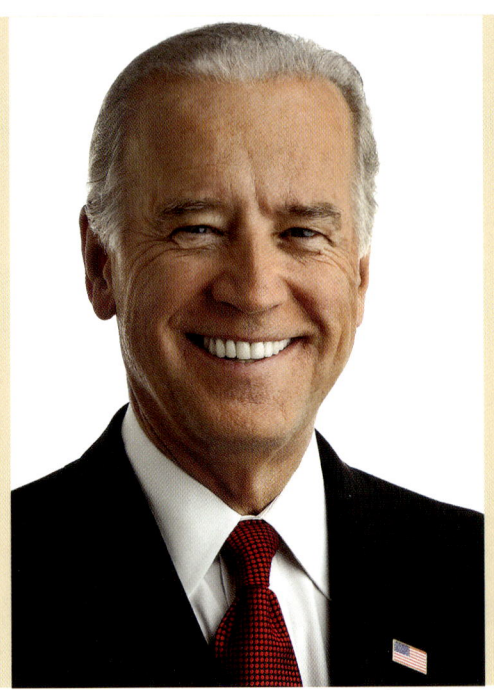

Kamala Harris
Vice president
2021-

The White House

Biden, Joe (1942-   ), a Democrat, was elected president of the United States in 2020. He had earlier served as vice president under President Barack Obama from 2009 to 2017 and had a long career in the U.S. Senate. In the 2020 presidential election, Biden and his running mate, Senator Kamala Harris of California, defeated the Republican incumbents, President Donald J. Trump and Vice President Mike Pence.

Prior to Biden's ascent to the presidency, he had been a son of Scranton, Pennsylvania, and an ambitious young lawmaker in Delaware. He had worked to overcome a childhood stutter and faced embarrassment for a plagiarism incident during a national campaign. He became known for the devastating losses that struck his family, and for his tough-and-tender "Uncle Joe" persona waging national election battles with Obama.

In the 2020 campaign for his party's nomination, Biden recovered after poor finishes in early nominating contests. In early spring, Biden built a sizable lead in pledged delegates over his closest rival, Senator Bernie Sanders of Vermont. Sanders, a leader of the party's progressive wing, pledged his support for Biden's candidacy in April, after the COVID-19 pandemic forced an end to traditional public campaign events.

COVID-19, a sometimes-fatal respiratory disease caused by a type of coronavirus, peaked in several northern U.S. cities in spring 2020 before later spiking in parts of the South and West. Many Americans were ordered to shelter at home, and state governors restricted social and business activities. Unemployment soared. Millions of Americans became infected with the virus, and thousands died. Trump sometimes downplayed the severity of the outbreak, and he cheered on protests against business restrictions. Some less partisan, or *swing,* voters began to wonder whether Trump's earlier presiding over a strong economy was now outweighed by his response to the COVID-19 crisis.

In late spring and summer, the deaths of African Americans at the hands of police officers sparked widespread protests. Trump largely ignored calls to address racial injustice. He portrayed himself as the law-and-order candidate who would protect Americans from riots, looting, and other lawless behavior that took place amid some protests. Biden criticized Trump's use of federal agents to aggressively disperse and arrest protesters in Portland, Oregon, and in Washington, D.C.

During the general election campaign, Biden told voters that the president had put American lives at risk by failing to maintain a consistent message during the pandemic. He also chided Trump for failing to encourage unity during periods of inflamed tensions between minority groups and police. Trump's campaign worked to label the 77-year-old Biden as infirm, politically radical, and corrupt. In November voting, Biden and Harris defeated Trump and Pence. Trump's refusal to accept the election loss, however, led to a riot, on Jan. 6, 2021, at the U.S. Capitol.

Important dates in Biden's life

1942 (Nov. 20) Born in Scranton, Pennsylvania.
1953 Biden family moves to Delaware.
1965 Graduated from the University of Delaware.
1966 (Aug. 22) Married Neilia Hunter.
1968 Graduated from the Syracuse University College of Law.
1970 Elected to the New Castle County Council.
1972 Elected to the U.S. Senate.
1972 (Dec. 18) Neilia and Amy Biden died.
1977 (June 17) Married Jill Jacobs.
2008 Elected vice president of the United States.
2012 Reelected vice president.
2020 Elected president of the United States.

Early life

Family background. Joseph Robinette Biden, Jr., was born in Scranton, Pennsylvania, on Nov. 20, 1942. He was the first of four children, followed by Valerie (1945-   ), a political strategist; Jim (1949-   ), an entrepreneur; and Frank (1953-   ), a real estate developer. Their parents were Joseph Robinette Biden, Sr. (1915-2002), and Catherine Eugenia Finnegan (called Jean) (1917-2010).

Biden's roots in Scranton went back generations. A maternal great-great-grandfather had been a state senator, and a great-grandfather had been an engineer who developed many of the city's streets. The family was Irish on his mother's side, and mostly English on his father's. Biden's English ancestors came to America in the early 1800's, settling in Maryland. Biden's mother's ancestors came from Ireland during the potato famine of the mid-1800's. Biden gained insight into his heritage during a 2016 state visit to Ireland while serving as vice president.

Boyhood. Biden often referred fondly to his childhood in Scranton. He recalled playing pick-up baseball games, seeing Western movies at the cinema, visiting with grandparents, and attending Roman Catholic Mass on Sundays.

Joe was popular among his peers. Friends recalled that he would never turn down a dare. But he struggled with a stuttering impediment. Classmates sometimes mocked him or called him cruel names. Joe's mother would comfort him. But she urged him to stand up to bullies, and Joe sometimes got into fistfights. A favorite uncle had also stuttered, and Joe had seen him lose confidence. Joe aimed to become a stronger speaker. He memorized passages of poetry and recited them in the mirror. He later often said that his difficulties helped him develop empathy for other people who struggle.

Biden's parents struggled financially through much of his childhood. The business career of Joe Biden, Sr., had had a promising start. He had bought expensive suits and driven flashy cars. But a series of setbacks left the elder Biden and his family trying to make ends meet. The family lived with Joe's maternal grandparents, the Finnegans, in Scranton's predominantly Irish Catholic Green Ridge neighborhood. By 1950, job opportunities in the area had become scarce following the closure of local coal mines and textile mills. Biden's father kept looking for work.

Biden's childhood was spent in Scranton, Pennsylvania, as the oldest of four children.

Years later, on the campaign trail, Joe would frequently mention his father's resiliency. "My dad always said, 'Champ, the measure of a man is not how often he is knocked down, but how quickly he gets up'," Biden said.

Delaware days. In 1953, the family moved from Scranton to a two-bedroom apartment in Claymont, Delaware, just northeast of Wilmington. Biden's father had found work cleaning boilers there, and he later managed a used-car dealership. The family often drove back to Scranton to see family on weekends and holidays.

The Bidens' home stood across the street from Archmere Academy, an exclusive Catholic preparatory school. The family couldn't afford to send Joe there. So Joe began painting fences, weeding gardens, and taking on other odd jobs around the school to help pay the tuition. The Bidens later moved to a single-family home in Wilmington.

Biden's school friends recalled that he often started conversations about civil rights and environmental issues. He grew taller and joined the baseball and football teams. He was a standout in football as a halfback and wide receiver, leading his undefeated team in scoring during his senior season. Described by classmates as bright and talkative, Biden was voted class president his junior and senior years.

College and law school. After graduating from prep school, Biden attended the University of Delaware. He joined the freshman football team, but his parents, upset with Joe's poor academic marks, made him quit the sport. By his own admission, Joe was more focused on socializing, playing pranks, and having lively debates in the dormitories than in attending class.

Biden's boyhood home was his maternal grandparents' house in the Green Ridge neighborhood of Scranton, Pennsylvania.

Outline

I. **Early life**
    A. Family background
    B. Boyhood
    C. Delaware days
    D. College and law school
II. **Early career**
III. **Biden's family**
IV. **Entry into politics**
    A. County councilman
    B. United States senator
    C. The 2008 election
V. **Vice president**
VI. **A brief-but-busy retirement**
VII. **2020 presidential campaign**
    A. The race for the nomination
    B. General election campaign

Biden's young family posed for a photo postcard during his first Senate campaign in 1972. Pictured are, *from left to right*, son Hunter, wife Neilia, daughter Amy, Biden, and son Beau.

Biden's first presidential campaign was short-lived. *From left to right*, son Hunter, wife Jill, daughter Ashley, and son Beau joined Biden at a rally at a Wilmington, Delaware, rail station.

Biden met Neilia Hunter, an education student at Syracuse University, while on a spring-break trip during his junior year. The pair became a couple, and Joe began to concentrate harder on his studies. In 1965, he earned a bachelor's degree with a double major in history and political science. He then joined Neilia in upstate New York, where he attended the College of Law at Syracuse University. Biden graduated in 1968. He again had been an indifferent student, however, graduating 76th of the 85 students in his law class.

Early career

After law school, Biden clerked for a Wilmington law firm. He passed the Delaware bar exam in 1969. He began working part-time as a public defender, taking on cases for poor clients. He also worked for another law firm before starting his own practice. Biden took little joy from practicing law. He saw the nation embroiled in conflict over civil rights and the Vietnam War, and he sought a future in politics.

Biden's family

Biden and Neilia Hunter (1942-1972) married in 1966, after Biden had become a law student at Syracuse. The couple had three children: Joseph III (called Beau) (1969-2015); Robert (called Hunter) (1970-   ); and Naomi (called Amy) (1971-1972).

In December 1972, soon after Biden was first elected to the Senate, his wife and daughter were killed in an automobile accident while on a shopping excursion for a Christmas tree. Biden's sons were badly injured in the accident but survived.

Biden remarried in 1977. His wife, Jill Jacobs (1951-   ), was an educator who became a professor of English. The couple have a daughter, Ashley (1981-   ).

In 2015, Biden's son Beau died at the age of 46. Beau Biden, who served two terms as Delaware attorney general, had been diagnosed with brain cancer.

Entry into politics

County councilman. Biden joined the Democratic Party while working as a young lawyer. In 1970, he won election to the New Castle County Council. He served on the council from 1970 to 1972.

United States senator. Local Democrats saw promise in Biden. In 1972, they encouraged him to mount a long-shot campaign against a popular Republican incumbent of the U.S. Senate. The 29-year-old Biden faced J. Caleb Boggs, a two-term senator and former Delaware governor, in the general election. Biden's sister served as campaign manager, and his father helped him conduct a door-to-door campaign. In November, Biden won an upset victory with a margin of only a few thousand votes. He turned 30—the minimum age for a senator—about two weeks after the election.

Delaware commute. Biden's Senate career began in January 1973, weeks after the deaths of his wife and daughter. His sons remained hospitalized at the time. Biden decided that he would continue to live in Wilmington to care for his sons and travel each day to Washington, D.C., for his work in the Senate. He was reelected in 1978 and every six years through 2008. For this train commute, which continued throughout his 36-year Senate career, Biden gained the nickname "Amtrak Joe."

Embarrassing setback. In June 1987, Biden began a campaign for the 1988 Democratic presidential nomination. Political observers considered him one of the party's stronger candidates. In September, however, news reports showed that, in a speech a month earlier in Iowa, he had *plagiarized* (quoted without attribution) the words of British politician Neil Kinnock. Biden had quoted Kinnock in earlier versions of the speech but omitted the attribution at the Iowa event. News stories also surfaced with accounts of Biden misstating his academic record. Biden soon ended his once-promising campaign. The incident humbled Biden and damaged his national reputation. But he remained committed to his Senate work and maintained his political popularity in his home state.

Judiciary Committee. Biden chaired the powerful Judiciary Committee from 1987 to 1995. In his first year as chairman, he won attention for his tough questioning of conservative Supreme Court nominee Robert Bork. The Senate later voted against Bork's nomination. In 1988, Biden suffered two brain *aneurysms*—that is, the weakening and swelling of arteries in the brain. He missed seven months in the Senate while recovering.

Biden had long courted supporters in poor minority communities, but he also sought the support of law enforcement personnel. In the late 1980's and early 1990's, public opinion polls showed that crime was a top concern for voters. In 1994, Biden guided the Senate passage of the Violent Crime Control and Law Enforcement Act, a major anticrime bill. The law included funding to hire 100,000 police officers, build new prisons, and conduct crime prevention programs in communities nationwide.

Biden later expressed regret that certain parts of the crime bill—particularly its "three-strikes" provision—came to contribute to devastating outcomes in minority communities. The provision called for mandatory minimum prison sentences for persons convicted of three felonies. It stripped judges of options to issue more lenient punishments. In the 15 years following the bill's passage, violent crime rates decreased—due to a variety of factors—but the number of Americans in prisons doubled. Biden continued to defend some of the act's provisions, including its restrictions on automatic-weapon purchases and its measures encouraging states to treat, rather than imprison, nonviolent drug-law offenders.

Legislative accomplishments. Biden was chairman of the Senate Foreign Relations Committee from 2001 to 2003 and from 2007 to 2009. As a regular member of the committee, he introduced antiterrorism legislation and worked with conservative Republicans to pass arms-control agreements. In his career, Biden also introduced the first Senate bill to address climate change and was a primary sponsor of the Violence Against Women Act. Because he was more a dealmaker than an ideologue, Biden's votes over the years on such issues as banking deregulation and welfare reform drew the ire of both liberal and conservative observers. Befitting his commuting nickname, Biden was also a strong supporter of public transportation projects. In 2007, prior to embarking upon a presidential campaign, Biden wrote a memoir, *Promises to Keep: On Life and Politics.*

The 2008 election. In January 2007, Biden began a campaign for the 2008 Democratic nomination for president. He dropped out of the race in January 2008, however, after a poor showing in the Iowa Democratic caucuses. Senator Barack Obama eventually outlasted Senator and former First Lady Hillary Rodham Clinton in a bruising and expensive contest for the nomination.

Obama placed Biden on his short list of vice-presidential options from the start. Biden initially declined to be considered for the position before reconsidering. Obama found the nearly two-decades-older Biden to be a voice of experience—particularly in foreign policy—with a compelling personal story. Biden proved a feisty campaigner who helped communicate the ticket's message to working-class white voters.

Vice president

In August 2008, at the Democratic National Convention in Denver, delegates nominated Biden to be Obama's running mate. Obama and Biden were to face Republican opponents Senator John McCain of Arizona and Alaska Governor Sarah Palin. After Biden sparred with Palin in an October debate, polls showed that voters valued the experience he could bring to the vice

© John Duricka, AP Photo

Biden chaired the Senate Judiciary Committee from 1987 to 1995. In this 1994 photo, Biden discusses a proposal that aimed to prevent crime by helping disadvantaged children.

© Jerome Delay, AP Photo

President Barack Obama and Vice President Joe Biden defeated former Massachusetts Governor Mitt Romney and his running mate, Representative Paul Ryan, in the November 2012 election. In this photo, Obama, Biden, and their families celebrate the Democrats' reelection victory at a Chicago gathering for supporters.

presidency. In November, Obama and Biden defeated McCain and Palin by a comfortable margin. Biden also stood for reelection as senator and won, but he resigned the seat before taking office as vice president.

Obama and Biden were renominated in 2012 at their party's convention in Charlotte, North Carolina. They faced former Massachusetts Governor Mitt Romney and U.S. Representative Paul Ryan of Wisconsin in the general election. Biden and Ryan held an animated vice presidential debate. Biden made headlines after calling his opponent's assertions "a bunch of malarkey." Biden's performance helped Obama and Biden in the polls, and they went on to defeat Romney and Ryan in November.

As vice president, Biden met with leaders around the world. He helped implement a $787-billion economic stimulus bill meant to shore up a U.S. economy struggling through a global economic slowdown. He spoke in favor of legal gay marriage, and he worked to bring an end to the Iraq War (2003-2011). Biden became known for his heartfelt speeches about coping with grief. His book *Promise Me, Dad: A Year of Hope, Hardship, and Purpose* (2017) recounted his experience of losing his son Beau to cancer. In 2016, Obama named Biden to lead the White House Cancer Moonshot. The program aimed to coordinate research activities and streamline the development of new cancer treatments.

In 2015, Biden explored mounting a campaign for the 2016 presidential nomination. Polls showed him in a tight contest with Hillary Clinton. Grieving the death of his son, however, he decided that the time was not right for campaigning. Clinton lined up support from Democratic officials, and Biden prepared for a career after politics.

A brief-but-busy retirement

Biden left the office of vice president in January 2017. In February, Joe and Jill Biden announced the creation of the Biden Foundation, which focused on a range of issues, including foreign policy, helping military families, and combating violence against women. They also formed the Biden Cancer Initiative, a nonprofit foundation building on the Obama administration's efforts to fight the disease while Biden served as vice president.

Biden was named to lead a University of Pennsylvania academic center focused on foreign policy and national security. He also led a University of Delaware program dedicated to domestic policy. The National Constitution Center in Philadelphia, Pennsylvania, named Biden its chairman. Biden recorded an audiobook, *Conversations With Joe* (2018), in which he discussed his family and career.

Trump's narrow upset, in 2016, of the favored Clinton threatened to undo many of the accomplishments of the Obama presidency. After Trump became president, Biden bristled at many of his statements and actions. He resolved to try to deny Trump a second term.

2020 presidential campaign

The race for the nomination. In April 2019, Biden announced that he would seek the Democratic Party's 2020 nomination for president of the United States. In his announcement, Biden warned of the dangers of white nationalism and declared that Trump posed a threat to the nation's values.

Rivalry and impeachment. Well before the 2020 campaign began, Trump's advisers had identified Biden as the president's likeliest opponent and worked to discredit him. Reports claimed that in July 2019, Trump, without presenting any evidence, repeatedly asked Ukraine President Volodymyr Zelensky to launch an investigation into what he called possible corruption involving Biden and his son Hunter. Hunter Biden had served on the board of directors of the Ukrainian energy company Burisma, and a conspiracy theory about the Bidens had developed among right-wing commentators.

In September 2019, the House of Representatives began an impeachment inquiry into Trump's actions regarding Ukraine. Reports alleged that Trump had instructed aides to withhold the transfer to Ukraine of about $400 million in military aid that Congress had approved. The report charged that Trump used the funds as leverage while insisting that Ukraine investigate the Bidens. Trump acknowledged that he had invited Ukraine to investigate the Bidens but insisted that his actions were not illegal.

In December, the House of Representatives approved two articles of impeachment: (1) abuse of power, for urging a foreign power to investigate a domestic political rival; and (2) obstruction of Congress, for impeding

© Olivier Douliery, AFP/Getty Images

The 2020 Democratic National Convention was held under unconventional circumstances in Milwaukee, Wisconsin, in August. Biden and his running mate, Senator Kamala Harris of California, *shown here,* accepted the party's nomination in a hall without in-person attendees during the ongoing COVID-19 pandemic.

investigators. Trump's impeachment trial in the Senate began in January 2020. In February, the Senate, voting almost entirely along party lines, acquitted President Trump of the charges.

Nomination contests. At the start of the nomination campaign, Biden consistently appeared at or near the top of opinion polls. Democratic candidates gathered for a series of debates beginning in June 2019. Biden's debate opponents frequently focused their attacks on the front-runner. Competitors for the nomination included Senators Elizabeth Warren of Massachusetts, Kamala Harris of California, Cory Booker of New Jersey, Amy Klobuchar of Minnesota, and Bernie Sanders of Vermont; U.S. Representative Tulsi Gabbard of Hawaii; Pete Buttigieg, mayor of South Bend, Indiana; and former New York City Mayor Michael Bloomberg.

In February 2020, Biden finished fourth in Iowa and fifth in New Hampshire, the first two nominating contests of the year. Sanders's campaign appeared to have the most momentum of any of the candidates. But Biden drew on the support of establishment Democratic officials, many of whom he had worked with for decades. His longtime contacts in African American communities helped bring out support in South Carolina and other states holding primaries. Later in the month, Biden had a bounce-back win in South Carolina. He pulled ahead in the delegate count after the voting on March 3—so-called Super Tuesday—but the race remained close. He extended his lead later in March. About that time, the COVID-19 pandemic curtailed traditional campaigning. Sanders ended his campaign in April, and Biden became the party's *presumptive* (likely) nominee. In June, Biden won enough delegates to officially secure the nomination.

Seasons of discord. COVID-19 caused major disruptions to life in the United States beginning in early 2020. State and local officials implemented business and social restrictions to safeguard public health. Congress passed, and Trump signed, measures to provide relief to unemployed workers and vulnerable businesses. Restrictions were lifted for some areas later in the spring, but deadly outbreaks continued to occur.

In the late spring and summer of 2020, the quiet of COVID-19 lockdowns gave way to loud and sustained protests against racial injustice. Demonstrations began in May, following the brutal video-documented death of an African American man, George Floyd, while he was in the custody of Minneapolis police. The shooting of Jacob Blake in Kenosha, Wisconsin, by police led to further protests in August.

Convention. In mid-August, prior to the Democratic National Convention, Biden named California Senator Kamala Harris to be his running mate. The convention took place in Milwaukee from August 17 to 20. Because of the ongoing pandemic, convention speeches occurred *virtually*—that is, via video transmission—without in-person attendees. Speakers included Michelle Obama, Bernie Sanders, and Hillary Clinton; and former Presidents Jimmy Carter, Bill Clinton, and Barack Obama. Republicans who attested to Biden's character included John Kasich, former governor of Ohio; former Secretary of State Colin Powell; and Cindy McCain, wife of the late Senator John McCain.

Biden accepted the nomination on August 20, when he asked voters, "with love and hope and light, [to] join in the battle for the soul of our nation." He urged Americans to act with compassion and decency, and he spoke of the urgency to protect democratic institutions against what he called Trump's abuses. Biden had worked with Sanders to craft proposals to appeal to the progressive wing of the party. The party's platform included helping Americans with child-care and elder-care expenses; expanding access to affordable housing; and investing in education, especially in poor communities. Biden also proposed to strengthen the Social Security program, enact reforms in the criminal justice system, and take steps toward universal health care coverage.

General election campaign. The race between Biden and Trump officially began in late August, after Trump and Pence were renominated to be the candidates of the Republican Party.

In campaign ads and speeches, Biden and Trump clashed fiercely over the Trump administration's response to the COVID-19 pandemic; claims of systemic racism and improper use of force by police; and international alliances and trade agreements. Political arguments also became personal. Biden called Trump the most divisive president in the nation's history. Trump said Biden was not fit for the challenges of the position.

For all the differences in their political philosophies and the circumstances of their upbringings, the candidates shared some commonalities. Both had gained recognition as teenage athletes and class leaders. Both were *teetotalers* (nondrinkers) who had seen family members succumb to alcohol addiction. And both candidates, born in the 1940's, would be the oldest ever to win election as president.

In late September, Biden and Trump participated in their first presidential debate. Days later, Trump announced that he had tested positive for COVID-19. He received treatment at Walter Reed National Military Medical Center before returning to the White House. Organizers proposed that a second debate, scheduled for October 15, be held virtually because of concerns about Trump's possible contagiousness. Trump declined to participate, however, and the two candidates appeared separately in televised "town hall" forums. A final in-person debate took place on October 22.

Biden defeated Trump in the November election, winning close races in a number of states. Trump's campaign filed dozens of lawsuits alleging electoral fraud, but judges ruled the challenges to be without merit. Trump continued to angrily insist the election had been stolen from him. On Jan. 6, 2021, pro-Trump protesters violently rioted at the U.S. Capitol while Congress was in session to affirm Biden's victory. Biden and Harris took office on Inauguration Day, January 21.   Kenneth J. Shenkman

Biden's election

Place of nominating convention	Milwaukee
Ballot on which nominated	1st
Republican opponent	Donald J. Trump
Electoral vote	306 (Biden) to 232 (Trump)
Popular vote	81,268,924 (Biden) to 74,216,154 (Trump)
Age at inauguration	78

INDEX

A
"accidental presidents", 42-43
Adams, John, 11, 41, 42, 50
Adams, John Quincy, 11, 13, 50, 52
African Americans, 4, 29
Agnew, Spiro T., 12
Amendment 12. See 12th Amendment
Angelou, Maya, 50
Arthur, Chester A., 11, 42
Article II, 12, 38

B
ballot, 26-27, 30-31, 33
Barr, William, 31
Biden, Joe, 4, 7, 11, 18, 19, 21, 23, 24, 42, 47, 48, 51
Bloomberg, Michael, 19
Bull Moose (political party), 18
Bush, George H. W., 11, 20, 42, 45, 47, 52
Bush, George W., 13, 35, 40, 47, 52
Bush v. Gore (lawsuit), 13
Buttigieg, Pete, 19

C
campaigning, 22-25
Carter, Jimmy, 11, 52
caucus, 14, 15, 18
Cheney, Richard B., 40
citizenship, 28
civil rights movement, 29
Cleveland, Grover, 11
Clinton, Bill, 10, 18, 39, 47, 52
computerized voting, 30
Constitution. See U.S. Constitution
convention: national, 14, 20-21, 23; Constitutional (1787), 38
Coolidge, Calvin, 42, 53
coronavirus, 5. See also COVID-19
COVID-19, 4, 19, 21, 23, 31, 33, 51
Curtis, Charles, 41
Cybersecurity and Infrastructure Security Agency (CISA), 33

D
"dark horse" candidate, 20
debates, 19, 24
delegates, 14, 17, 20, 26, 34
democracy, 29, 37
Democratic National Committee (DNC), 19
Democratic Party, 17-18, 24
donkey (symbol), 17

E
Eisenhower, Dwight D., 16, 42, 43
Election Day, 26-33
Electoral College, 13, 14-15, 26, 34-37, 41
elephant (symbol), 17

F
Federalist, No. 10, The, 25
Ferraro, Geraldine, 45
Fillmore, Millard, 42
fireside chats, 9
Florida, 13, 35
Ford, Gerald R., 12, 42

Founding Fathers, 41
Franklin, Benjamin, 38
Frost, Robert, 50

G
Gabbard, Tulsi, 19
Garfield, James A., 23, 42
general election, 14
Georgia, 45
Gore, Al, 13, 35
Gorman, Amanda, 50
Grant, Ulysses S., 52

H
Harding, Warren G., 23, 52
Harris, Kamala, 21, 44-45
Harrison, Benjamin, 11, 23, 35
Harrison, William Henry, 49
Hayes, Rutherford B., 35, 53

I
impeachment, 5, 10-11, 38-39
Inauguration Day, 48-51
Iowa caucus, 18

J
Jackson, Andrew, 17
Jefferson, Thomas, 13, 41, 42, 49
Johnson, Andrew, 10, 11, 39, 42, 50, 52
Johnson, Lady Bird, 49
Johnson, Lyndon B., 42, 43, 49, 50

K
Kennedy, John F., 9, 11, 24, 42, 43
Klobuchar, Amy, 19

L
Lame Duck Amendment. See 20th Amendment
Lewis, John, 29
libraries. See presidential libraries
Lincoln, Abraham, 6, 29, 53

M
Madison, James, 25
mail-in voting, 26-27, 30-31, 33
McConnell, Mitch, 39
McKinley, William, 11, 23, 53
Mondale, Walter F., 45

N
NASA, 26
Nast, Thomas, 17
National Archives and Records Administration (NARA), 53
natural-born citizen, 10, 14
naturalization, 28
New Hampshire primary, 18
Nixon, Richard M., 10, 12, 24, 38, 42, 43, 50

O
Obama, Barack, 46, 47, 49, 52, 53

P
pandemic. See COVID-19

62

Pelosi, Nancy, 43, 45
Pence, Mike, 34, 36, 43
Pierce, Franklin, 11
political parties, 17, 41
Polk, James K., 20
polling places, 26-27, 30; challenging, 33; watching, 26, 33
popular vote, 26, 35
president (United States), 6-11, 52-53; duties and roles, 8-9; oath, 48; qualifications, 10, 14; salary, 10; terms, 10
presidential libraries, 53
Presidential Succession Act, 12-13
presidential transition, 46-47
Presidential Transition Act, 46
primary, 14-15, 18
Progressive Party, 18
protests, 4, 25; civil rights, 31; state capitols, 51; U.S. Capitol, 36-37, 51

R
Reagan, Ronald, 10, 34, 42, 45, 47, 49
representative democracy, 17, 29
Republican Party, 17
Roberts, John G., 4, 49, 51
Roosevelt, Eleanor, 43
Roosevelt, Franklin D., 9, 11, 43, 49, 53
Roosevelt, Theodore, 11, 18, 42

S
Sanders, Bernie, 19
Sanford, Mark, 19
Selma, Alabama, 29
Sotomayor, Sonia, 44
Steyer, Tom, 19
suffrage, 28

T
Taft, William Howard, 11, 52
transition. *See* presidential transition

Truman, Harry S., 7, 42, 43
Trump, Donald J., 4-5, 9, 10, 11, 19, 21, 23, 24, 33, 35, 36, 42, 46, 47, 50, 51; impeachment, 5, 10, 38-39; voter fraud claims, 31
12th Amendment, 12-13, 41
20th Amendment, 12-13, 46, 49
25th Amendment, 42-43
22nd Amendment, 10, 11
26th Amendment, 28
2020 election: national conventions, 21, 23; COVID-19, 19, 21, 23, 31, 33; cost, 24; debates, 24; divisiveness, 25; Electoral College certification, 36-37; legal challenges, 31, 33; poll watching, 33; primary candidates, 19; results, 5, 32; security, 33
Twitter, 9
Tyler, John, 42

U
U.S. Capitol, 5, 39, 42, 43, 48, 51; protests, 36-37
U.S. Constitution, 7, 10, 25, 28, 40; Article II, 12, 38. *See also individual amendments*
U.S. House of Representatives, 10, 13, 34, 38-39, 43, 52
U.S. Senate, 10, 40, 45, 52
U.S. Supreme Court, 13, 35

V
Van Buren, Martin, 11, 20, 42, 50
vice president, 12, 40-45
voting, 26-33; qualifications, 28; registration, 28

W
Walsh, Joe, 19
War of 1812, 37
Warren, Elizabeth, 19
Washington, George, 17, 49
Weld, William, 19
Wilson, Woodrow, 42, 53

WEBSITES

Federal Election Commission
http://www.fec.gov/
Official website of the Federal Election Commission.

National Archives Presidential Libraries and Museums
http://www.archives.gov/presidential-libraries/
The official site for Presidential Libraries and Museums in the National Archives.

Office of the President
https://www.whitehouse.gov/administration/president-biden/
Official White House site of United States President.

The Presidents of the United States
https://www.whitehouse.gov/about-the-white-house/presidents/
Biographical information on the presidents from the official site of the White House.

The White House Historical Association
https://www.whitehousehistory.org/
Official site of the White House Historical Association. Features history of the White House, including architecture, gardens and grounds, and historical information on the U.S. presidents, first ladies, and first families who have lived there.

ACKNOWLEDGMENTS

Cover	© Zack Stock Photo/Shutterstock; © Danny Green, Nature Picture Library; © Andamanec/Shutterstock
1	© Caroline Purser, Getty Images
3	The White House
4-5	© Roman Babakin, Shutterstock
6-7	© Shutterstock; Harry S. Truman Library
8-9	White House Historical Association; © NBC; © Keystone/Getty Images; © Saul Loeb, AFP/Getty Images
10-11	© Dirck Halstead, The LIFE Images Collection/Getty Images; National Portrait Gallery, Smithsonian Institution; © Bettmann/Getty Images
12-13	Pete Souza, White House; © Dirck Halstead, The LIFE Images Collection/Getty Images; © Harry Hamburg, NY Daily News Archive/Getty Images
14-15	Ifrah Syed, USAGov
16-17	© George Tames, The New York Times/Redux Pictures; © PeskyMonkey/Shutterstock
18-19	© Paul J. Richards, AFP/Getty Images; © Robyn Beck, AFP/Getty Images
20-21	© Philip Gould, Corbis/Getty Images; © Stefani Reynolds, Bloomberg/Getty Images; © Erin Scott, Polaris/Bloomberg/Getty Images
22-23	© Shutterstock; © Rachel Mummey, Bloomberg/Getty Images; Adam Schultz, Biden for President; Smithsonian Institution
24-25	© Bettmann/Getty Images; © Shutterstock; White House Historical Association; Public Domain; NPS
26-27	© Seth Herald, AFP/Getty Images; Public Domain
28-29	© Allen J. Schaben, Los Angeles Times/Getty Images; © Shutterstock; © Chip Somodevilla, Getty Images
30-31	© Hill Street Studios/Getty Images; © David Paul Morris, Bloomberg/Getty Images
32-33	© Ethan Miller, Getty Images; The White House; WORLD BOOK map; © Elijah Nouvelage, Bloomberg/Getty Images
34-35	© Kevin Dietsch, Getty Images
36-37	© Lev Radin, Shutterstock; © Tasos Katopodis, Getty Images; Library of Congress
38-39	*Scene at the Signing of the Constitution of the United States* (1940), oil on canvas by Howard Chandler Christy; U.S. Capitol Building; © Bill Pierce, The LIFE Images Collection/Getty Images; © Sarah Silbiger, Getty Images
40-41	© Smith Collection/Gado/Getty Images; Library of Congress
42-43	Public Domain (Lyndon B. Johnson Library); © Universal History Archive/Universal Images Group/Getty Images
44-45	© Kent Nishimura, Los Angeles Times/Getty Images; Kamala Harris Campaign
46-47	Pete Souza, White House; © Amadeustx/Shutterstock; George H.W. Bush Presidential Library and Museum; George W. Bush Presidential Library and Museum
48-49	© Jonathan Newton, The Washington Post/Getty Images; US Capitol
50-51	© Rolls Press/Popperfoto/Getty Images; © Rob Carr, Getty Images; © Stephanie Keith, Getty Images
52-53	© Mandel Ngan, AFP/Getty Images
54-55	The White House; White House Historical Association

★ ★ ★ ★ ★ ★ ★ ★ ★ ★ ★ ★ ★ ★

Answers to questions on page 55

1. George Washington
2. Gerald R. Ford
3. Grover Cleveland
4. Lyndon B. Johnson
5. William H. Taft
6. Richard M. Nixon and Joe Biden
7. John F. Kennedy, in 1961
8. William H. Harrison, one month, 1841
9. Franklin D. Roosevelt, 12 years, 1 month, 8 days
10. Ronald Reagan, in 1984, 525 electoral votes
11. Rutherford B. Hayes, in 1876; Benjamin Harrison, in 1888; George W. Bush, in 2000; and Donald J. Trump, in 2016
12. Richard M. Nixon, in 1974
13. Theodore Roosevelt, 42
14. John F. Kennedy, 43
15. Joe Biden, 77 years and 349 days when he was elected in 2020
16. Andrew Johnson, Bill Clinton, Donald J. Trump
17. Donald J. Trump
18. Jimmy Carter
19. John Quincy Adams was elected to the U.S. House of Representatives in 1830; Andrew Johnson was elected to the U.S. Senate in 1875
20. George Washington
21. Thomas Jefferson
22. William H. Harrison
23. Franklin D. Roosevelt
24. George W. Bush
25. James K. Polk
26. Franklin D. Roosevelt and Barack Obama
27. Thomas Jefferson, in 1801; and John Quincy Adams, in 1825
28. Theodore Roosevelt, the Bull Moose Party, in 1912
29. John F. Kennedy and Richard M. Nixon, in 1960
30. Bill Clinton, in 1992; and Joe Biden, in 2020

Children's 324.63 DES
Destination
Pennsylvania Avenue :

12/23/21